Arena-Taschenbuch

Band 2449

Andreas Schlüter,
geboren 1958, ist einer der erfolgreichsten Jugendbuchautoren der letzten Jahre. Mit seinem Kinderroman »Level 4 – Die Stadt der Kinder« hatte er vom Start weg großen Erfolg und eine riesige Leserschar. Bevor Andreas Schlüter zum Schreiben kam, leitete er mehrere Jahre Kinder- und Jugendgruppen in Hamburg. Seit 1990 arbeitet er als freischaffender Journalist und Redakteur, seit 1996 als freier Schriftsteller.

Von Andreas Schlüter sind als Arena-Taschenbuch erschienen:
Schnappschuss! (Band 2450)
Abgezockt! (Band 2452)

Andreas Schlüter

Level 4

Kid City

Ins Englische übersetzt von Anthea Bell

Didaktische Bearbeitung: Birgit Hock

Arena

In neuer Rechtschreibung

1. Auflage dieser Ausgabe als Arena-Taschenbuch 2004
Die Erstausgabe erschien 1994 unter dem Titel *Level 4. Die Stadt der Kinder*
bei Altberliner, Berlin/München.

Englische Fassung: Anthea Bell

Umschlagillustration: Caroline Kehr
Umschlagtypografie: knaus. büro für konzeptionelle und visuelle identitäten,
Würzburg
Gesamtherstellung: Westermann Druck Zwickau GmbH
ISSN 0518-4002
ISBN 3-401-02449-3

The New Computer Game

The sun shone through the window right into Ben's eyes. Ben blinked, **squinted** at his radio alarm, and next moment he was wide awake. The clock showed sixthirty. He could really have slept in for another half an hour if he'd wanted, but today he just couldn't do that.

Full of excitement, Ben jumped out of bed. Today was *the* day. Today he was finally getting that new computer game. His best friend Frank was going to bring it to school. In return Ben had promised him the new **tracksuit** that Grandma had given him. It was a steep price to pay. Just for a moment Ben had **misgivings**: ought he really to do the deal? His grandmother certainly wouldn't be pleased to know he was planning **to swap** the tracksuit for a computer game. But he'd thought it all over for two weeks and made his decision. The computer game mattered more to him.

Ben dressed **at the speed of light**. He opened his chest of drawers and **snatched** two socks, one red and one green. Now, quick, sweater and jeans. Minutes later he put his head around the door of his mother's bedroom. »Hi, Mum! No breakfast today?«

Ben's mother shot upright in bed. She gave the alarm clock a **frantic** glance. Six thirty-three. Thank heavens, she hadn't overslept after all.

»Ben!« she said in surprise. »Look, it's only six thirty.

(to) squint: schielen

tracksuit: der Trainingsanzug

misgivings: die Bedenken

(to) swap: tauschen

at the speed of light: mit Lichtgeschwindigkeit

(to) snatch: greifen

frantic: hektisch, verzweifelt

Another forty-five minutes to breakfast. What's up with you?«

in urgent tones: mit drängeliger Stimme

(to) groan: stöhnen

grouchily: grantig

(to) inquire: nachfragen, sich erkundigen

waist: die Taille

flies (*pl*): der Hosenschlitz

baffled: verblüfft

indignantly: entrüstet, empört

awkward: unangenehm

»I have to be at school early today,« Ben told her **in urgent tones**. »I'm getting a new computer game.«

»I don't believe it!« **groaned** Ben's mother, letting her head drop back on the warm, soft pillow. . . »You wake me up half an hour early to tell me that?»

»Well, it's important,« said Ben **grouchily**.

»Oh, sure,« said his mother, slowly sitting up in bed again. She looked at Ben again and suddenly laughed out loud.

»What's the joke?« Ben **inquired**.

Shaking her head, his mother looked at the red sock and the green sock. Her eyes moved on to the **waist** of Ben's jeans, saw that his **flies** were still open, travelled still higher and noticed that his sweater was on back to front.

»You clown, have you looked at yourself in the mirror today?« asked his mother, giggling. »I bet the game was so important you didn't even wash.«

Wash! I ask you! I'm getting the new computer game today and she carries on about washing! Ben was **baffled**. *I washed last night, I slept in a clean bed and I got out of that clean bed again this morning. So can anyone tell me how I'd be dirty?*

»I'm not a baby any more,« said Ben **indignantly**, hoping to get away from the **awkward** subject of washing as soon as possible.

»Of course not,« agreed his mother, grinning. »Still, it

seems you're not big enough yet to get dressed properly, let along make your own breakfast.«

»Oh, Ma!« **groaned** Ben. »You never take me seriously. Look, it's nearly ten to seven. I must go.«

»It's not even twenty to seven,« his mother corrected him. »Must be a really important game to get you up so early.« She sat on the edge of the bed, rubbed her eyes sleepily again and picked up her dressing-gown from the floor beside the bed. »Where's this wonderful game coming from?« she asked.

»Frank,« said Ben at once. »It's a **swap**.« As soon as he said it he wished he hadn't.

Now she'll ask what I'm swapping for it. He **made a beeline for** the kitchen. Sure enough, here came the question he expected. »A swap? What for?«

Ben **pretended** he hadn't heard. His mother **shuffled** into the kitchen and asked again as she took milk, butter and jam out of the fridge.

Ben **took refuge in** his room. »I have to pack up my things for school,« he said as **casually** as possible.

As he entered his room, his radio alarm was just going off. It was set for quarter to seven. Some man reading the news summary was **droning on**. »The following measures **to counter** the escalation of street violence are therefore being discussed by parliamentary committees.« Ben pressed the Off button. *All that boring talk*, he thought. *Who bothers about it?*

He picked up his school bag, hoping it had the books

(to) groan: stöhnen

swap: der Tausch

(to) make a beeline for sb/sth: schnell, geradewegs auf jdn/etw zugehen

(to) pretend: vortäuschen, vorgeben; so tun, als ob
(to) shuffle: schlurfen

(to) take refuge in: sich flüchten
casually: beiläufig, lässig

(to) drone on: leiern
(to) counter: bekämpfen, entgegenwirken

he'd need today in it. Over the last three days he'd been lucky anyway with the basic stuff in his bag. An exercise book, two pens, and of course his maths and physics books. Ben always had those with him. He wasn't about to miss out on his favourite subjects. His history textbook, on the other hand, had **vanished without trace** three weeks ago, but no one at school had noticed yet.

(to) vanish without trace: spurlos verschwinden

He went back into the kitchen, where his mother had now laid a good breakfast just as she did every morning. Her coffee was still **gurgling** through the filter machine. Ben drank his glass of milk in a single gulp, took an apple from the fruit bowl and disappeared into the front hall.

(to) gurgle: gluckern

»Don't you want any breakfast?« asked his mother in surprise.

» . . .ised . . . eet . . . nk,« **grunted** Ben, holding the apple in his mouth as he put his jacket on, at the same time trying to get his right foot into a **trainer** that **was** still **laced up**.

(to) grunt: grunzen, brummen, knurren

trainer: der Sportschuh

to be laced up: zugeschnürt sein

»What?« asked his mother.

Removing the apple from his mouth, Ben repeated impatiently, »I promised to meet Frank. And it's so late already.«

He finally managed to get his trainers on without unlacing them first. Picking up his school bag, he grabbed the sandwich his mother was handing him and was about to hurry out of the door.

No luck – she was asking that question again. »Right,

so you're swapping this computer game with Frank? What for?«

He really did have to leave now. »My tracksuit,« he said very quickly, hoping his mother wouldn't hear him properly. But she did.

»The new tracksuit Grandma gave you?« she **insisted**.

»Yes,« Ben admitted in a small voice.

»Do you think that's a nice thing to do?« asked his mother, adding, »You wanted it so much. And Grandma went all over the place to find exactly the right tracksuit for you.«

»I know,« **mumbled** Ben, staring at the floor with his head bent. »But . . . well, I'm not all that mad about sport anyway. And this computer game isn't just any old game. It's really new and exciting. No one's ever made it to Level Four yet. When we're trying it in the store they always **chuck us out** before we can get that far, and . . .«

Ben's mother interrupted her son's sudden **torrent of words**. »It was the same with the other five hundred computer games, am I right?« Sometimes his mother just wouldn't let go.

»Only a hundred and forty-eight,« Ben put her right. He knew exactly how many games he had. »But I copied most of them. You can't copy this one!« Ben tried desperately to find good reasons why his grandmother's present of the tracksuit had to go.

»Well, it's *your* tracksuit,« said his mother. »You can do what you like with it. All I say is, be honest about

(to) insist: beharren, bestehen auf

(to) mumble: murmeln

(to) chuck sb out: jdn rausschmeißen

torrent of words: der Wortschwall

it. If Grandma asks you where the tracksuit is you must tell her **truthfully** what you did. So think about that for a moment.«

truthfully: ehrlich

»Yes, yes, I will,« promised Ben, hoping his grandmother would never ask any such question.

Barely ten minutes later Ben arrived at the school gates, out of breath. He'd run all the way, of course. His excitement grew with every step he took. He was going to get that new computer game **at last**. Long before he reached the school gates Ben was looking in all directions, hoping to spot Frank. But Frank was nowhere to be seen, and he wasn't at the school gates either. *I don't believe it*, thought Ben, looking at his watch, which showed that it was 14.15 hours in Tokyo, 1.15 in New York, 9.15 in Moscow and 7.15 here at Ben's school. He hadn't fixed to meet Frank until seven-thirty. *But you don't have to leave it to the very last minute*, he told his **absent** friend. Ben was getting more and more impatient.

barely: kaum, knapp

at last: endlich

absent: abwesend, nicht da

»Hi, Ben,« someone called across the school yard. Ben turned and saw Thomas **mooching** towards him. *That's all I needed*, thought Ben. *School will be out before that* ***dawdler*** *gets here*.

(to) mooch: schleichen, zockeln

dawdler: der Trödler, der Bummelant

»Have your done your maths homework? I need to copy it from somewhere,« shouted Thomas while he was still some way off. Two teachers hurrying past glanced at him in surprise. Maths was the first lesson, but even that didn't seem to make Thomas feel he'd better get a move on. He was approaching Ben in slow motion, as usual. Thomas thought that if you were in too much of a hurry you missed out on the best things in life. He was a **keen** collector of all kinds of **odds and ends**, never mind what they were. »The main thing is, they're for free and you only have to pick them up,« Thomas explained to his friends whenever he made another find. His room at home looked like the biggest, untidiest, craziest **lost property office** in town – the collection had even taken over his parents' garage.

»Watch out!« Ben instinctively jumped aside. Tyres **squealing**, a bike had braked right next to him just outside the school gates. It was a miracle it managed to stop before hitting them. Ben's heart was **thudding**. He gasped for air. Then he sighed with **relief**.

»Frank – at last! Where've you been all this time?«

»It was my mother. You know what it's like – eat your toast, drink your milk, are you sure you have everything for school, where's this, where's that . . .«

»Yes, just like mine,« Ben interrupted his friend. »Well – do you have it with you?«

»Of course. What did you think?« Frank fished a large bundle of newspaper out of his jacket pocket. **Relishing** Ben's happy **anticipation** to the full, Frank unfolded the newspaper very slowly, with **solemn** gestures and a **grave** face, as if about to reveal the greatest invention of the century to the world – even though it was only the new computer game that his father had passed on to him. Ben often envied Frank

keen: eifrig, begeistert
odds and ends (*pl*): Der Krimskram, der Kram

lost property office: das Fundbüro

(to) squeal: quietschen, quieken, kreischen

(to) thud: klopfen, pochen
relief: die Erleichterung

(to) relish: auskosten, Gefallen finden, genießen
anticipation: die Vorfreude
solemn: feierlich
grave: ernst

because his father, who worked for a computer firm, could get his hands on the very latest games. A father who could provide all these good things was **wasted** on Frank. First, Frank was more interested in sport than computers, and second, he usually failed right at the start on Level One in most games.

(to) waste: verschwenden, vergeuden

Something enclosed in yellow plastic foam and red rubber bands came into view.

»Do you have that maths homework or don't you?« Thomas had arrived by now.

»You're a pain, Thomas,« said Ben and Frank **in the same breath**. Thomas froze, not that you'd really have noticed since he usually moved so slowly anyway. *There's some mystery about this*, he guessed. But no one was about to tell him what it was, so he turned and mooched off again in the direction of the classroom.

in the same breath: im selben Atemzug

Frank had undone the plastic foam and rubber bands. But there was still another layer of wrapping – this time it was aluminium foil.

»Didn't you have a proper case for it at home?« complained Ben nervously.

»Nope. Better ask Thomas. He's sure to have one,« replied Frank, and went calmly on with unpacking the game. There was cotton wool under the foil, a **duster** under the cotton wool, a handkerchief under the duster, and under the handkerchief – at long last – was the CD-ROM with the game he wanted so much. Ben had often seen that game in the department store, he'd tried it out himself several times. But

duster: das Staubtuch

whenever he was about to reach the most **advanced** level some **spoilsport** salesman would come along and stop the fun. »You've been playing long enough,« he'd tell Ben. »The customers who are really going to buy want to see how it works.« Well, Ben couldn't care less about any salesman now.

advanced: fortgeschritten, anspruchsvoll
spoilsport: der Spielverderber, die Spielverderberin

»So where's the tracksuit?« asked Frank.

Ben carefully put the silver disk in the **sleeve** he'd brought with him. Then he pointed to the cardboard box he had brought to school, too. Frank picked it up, grinning happily.

sleeve: die Hülle

»Do me a favour,« Ben asked. »If you ever happen to meet my grandma don't tell her all about your new tracksuit, right?«

During lessons Ben couldn't concentrate at all, even in maths. He kept imagining himself reaching Level Four and successfully ending the game there with maximum points, a record score. He was so lost in thought that he didn't even notice a small, screwed-up ball of paper thrown at him from the right-hand side of the classroom. It landed on the floor right beside his chair.

Thomas **thumped** him on the back from behind.

(to) thump: klopfen, schlagen

»Note for you,« he whispered.

»Note? Where from?« asked Ben.

Thomas was grinning all over his face. »Where do you think?« he replied. »Same as usual.« He nodded briefly in Jennifer's direction.

Jennifer, sitting on the other side of the classroom by

the windows, was looking impatiently at Ben and wondering if he was ever going to notice her note – before the teacher did, anyway.

(to) smooth: glätten, glatt streichen

Ben **smoothed** out the crumpled paper and read:

Hi, Ben!

I haven't even looked at the maths homework properly yet.

And the maths test is tomorrow.

Can you help me?

This afternoon, please.

It's really important.

Jennifer.

(to) tick off: abhaken
anxious: begierig auf

That was all Ben needed. He himself had already **ticked off** preparation for the test on his To Do list. Or rather, he was so **anxious** to get started on the new computer game that he'd forgotten all about the test. That didn't matter. Ben had no problems with maths. He'd never had worse than a Two Minus in a test, even without any preparation for it.

Now here was Jennifer wanting help. And without *her* help his last English test would certainly have been a **disaster**. The fact was, **he owed her**.

disaster: die Katastrophe, das Fiasko
(to) owe sb sth: jdm etw schuldig sein
(to) tear: reißen, ausreißen
(to) scribble: kritzeln

Although he wasn't best pleased, Ben **tore** a page out of his exercise book and **scribbled** on it:

Hi, Jennifer!

Okay.

Come round to my place at four.

We'll go through the maths together.

But I don't have much time. Sorry, but I really don't.

Ben.

Ben folded up the note, wrote »Jennifer« on it in large letters, and sent it back by what they called the usual mailing route – the note was passed from hand to hand under the desks until it finally reached Jennifer.
She unfolded the paper, glanced through it, and a smile of relief spread over her face.
»Great,« she signalled to Ben with her thumb and forefinger in **sign language**. Ben rolled his eyes toward the ceiling, and then let his head drop heavily into his hands, elbows propped on the desk. That was his afternoon gone, he knew.

sign language: die Zeichensprache

The Game Begins

Ben was finally home.
He raced up to his room, **flung** his school bag into the corner and took the CD-ROM out of its sleeve. His hands were shaking, partly with excitement, partly because he'd run all the way from school. Still breathing heavily, he put the CD in its **slot**. With a swift gesture, Ben swept everything off his desk that might **distract** him as he played. Then he switched the computer on. The screen **flickered**. A brief **beep**. The usual standard lines came up on the screen in yellow and disappeared again. Ben began installing the game. Finally a shrill, simple **tune** was heard. Then the screen announced:

(to) fling: schleudern
slot: der Schlitz, das Fach
(to) distract: ablenken
(to) flicker: flimmern
beep: der Piepser, das Tuten
tune: die Melodie

KID CITY

Adventure Supergame from Computergames Inc.

followed by the rest of the usual **stuff:**

This game is protected by copyright. Order from . . ..

and so on.

»Oh, get on with it!« Ben shouted at the computer. Finally the screen showed a shopping street. Little figures were going into the stores and coming out again, always following the same **pattern** of movement. Two cars were **weaving** back and forth along the street in opposite directions. The figure that Ben could move with the joystick was in the bottom left-hand corner. He tried out the movements: left, right, forward (on the screen that was up), backward. Good, he could go on. Now he had to concentrate.

Up the street for a start, into the last shop. Joystick forward. Watch out for those cars, they're driven by kids with no driving licence. So their movements were **unpredictable**. Suddenly a flowerpot fell from the second building. It hit the road right beside the little figure and smashed – thousands of tiny dots of light scattered in all directions over the screen.

That was a close thing. In his excitement Ben had quite forgotten that the chaos in the city created these **sneaky** little **traps**. He'd have to go more carefully, because it was still a long way to Level Four. It was a shame you couldn't **skip** the early, easier levels of the game. You had to go right back to the beginning after every badly wrong move. Ben had played this opening

stuff: das Zeug

pattern: das Muster

(to) weave: sich schlängeln

unpredictable: unvorhersehbar

sneaky: gewieft, raffiniert

trap: die Falle

(to) skip: überspringen, auslassen

level of the game any number of times before, but he kept forgetting little details like the flowerpot.
This time he'd been lucky. *Into the shop*. The picture switched to a new scene: inside the shop. A **sinister** figure stood behind the **counter**. Ben knew this was no ordinary salesman, but a magician **in disguise** – one of the last grown-ups in the city. He must go carefully. He had to think hard about every step the figure he was operating took on its way to the glass case with the key in it – the key to the next level. And as Ben knew from his many attempts in the department store, there was a **trapdoor** in the floor just waiting for any incautious move the figure made.
Ben gripped the joystick firmly. And then – »Rrring! Rrring!« It was his own front door bell.
»I don't believe it!« groaned Ben. But a glance at his radio alarm brought him down to earth. It was four o'clock, so that must be Jennifer coming about the maths test.
Reluctantly, Ben rose from his chair. He slowly took a few steps towards the door of his room, never taking his eyes off the screen for a moment. Who knew what mean trick the magician would play on the figure in the game if it stood around in the same place too long? »Rrring!« went the **insistent** door bell.
»Just coming!« shouted Ben **crossly**. He hurried to the door, flung it open, barked out a brief »Hi!« and rushed straight back to his room. Jennifer's **jaw** dropped as she stood in the doorway.

sinister: finster, unheimlich
counter: der Ladentisch, die Theke
in disguise: verkleidet
trapdoor: die Falltür
reluctantly: widerwillig
insistent: hartnäckig
crossly: böse, verärgert, ärgerlich
jaw: der Kiefer, die Kinnlade

»So what was all that about?« asked Miriam. She was Jennifer's best friend, and after school she'd decided it would be a good idea to come along too. Maths wasn't her own best subject either. And an afternoon with Jennifer was always good fun, even if you were preparing for a maths test.

haste: die Hast, die Eile

In his **haste**, Ben hadn't even noticed that they were both there. They followed him slowly to his room. What a sight! A heap of computer magazines lay untidily on the floor. It was the biggest pile of paper Jennifer had ever seen in anyone's room, and it was surrounded by screwdrivers, **soldering irons**, wires, screws, **circuit diagrams** and **electric plugs**. The remains of a model electric motorway wound through this untidy **assortment** of spare parts, until it came up against a mountain bike standing upside down, obviously waiting to get its back wheel replaced. Jennifer saw that it was going to have to wait some time, because the back wheel was now in use as a mobile tripod for a home-made telescope, which stood beside an old black and white TV set with the back off it. Jennifer hardly dared step anywhere – it would be only too easy **to tread** on some electrical **component**. So she stood motionless in the doorway, wondering how they were going to do any maths in all this confusion.

soldering iron: der Lötkolben
circuit diagram: der Schaltplan
electric plug: die Steckdose
assortment: Ansammlung

(to) tread: treten
component: das Teil

Miriam wasn't bothered. She leaned on the back of Ben's chair, looked over his shoulder and watched the screen with interest. Miriam liked games herself and was always quick to catch on.

»Oh, **darn**!« said Ben crossly. »I don't believe it!«
»What's the matter?« asked Miriam, admiring Ben's speed as he hit the keys.
Ben was red in the face with annoyance. At a loss, he looked from Miriam to Jennifer and back again. Finally he **heaved** a deep **sigh** and said, **gloomily**, »The magician's **disappeared**!«

darn: verflixt

(to) heave: aussto-ßen
sigh: der Seufzer
gloomily: nieder-geschlagen
(to) disappear: verschwinden

A Terrible Discovery

Ben's mind wasn't on what he was doing. Jennifer had insisted it was time they got around to her maths, and Ben went along with her. But he couldn't stop thinking of the computer game. *Why wasn't it working? The magician had never disappeared in the middle of the game before, bringing it to a sudden end.* However often he switched the computer off, re-started it and loaded the game again, the errors just got even worse. Now it wasn't only the magician who had disappeared, there were no more cars on screen either. Only the little figure **steered** by the joystick was still hopping about in its computer world. Nothing was working any more. The game had frozen.
»Hi, Ben, how does this exercise go? You're not listening to me,« **complained** Jennifer. »I thought we were going to study for the test together."
»Yes, you're not explaining it properly,« Miriam told him, beginning to get fretful too. If they weren't

(to) steer: lenken, steuern

(to) complain: sich beklagen

playing the game any more, which was fun, she might at least prepare for the maths test. But obviously there wasn't much hope of that. Ben just muttered some incomprehensible **equations**, with one eye on his computer.

equation: die Gleichung (Math.)

»I'm going to get Frank to give back my tracksuit,« he said finally. »This game is useless.«

»Oh, for goodness' sake!« groaned the girls in unison.

All this was getting Jennifer down. »You and your stupid computer game!« she said crossly. »We might as well give up on the maths, I suppose. Come on, Miriam, we're off. He's no use to us today.«

»Okay,« Miriam agreed with her friend. »I'll just see if my parents are home yet. If not we might go for an ice somewhere, right?« And Miriam was on the way to the phone. A minute later she was back.

»Nobody home,« she said.

»Good, then let's go,« Jennifer decided, taking a step toward the door of the room. A crunching sound stopped her in her tracks.

»Watch out!« said Ben crossly. »Now you've trodden on my **photoelectric beam**!«

photoelectric beam: die Lichtschranke

»So how's anyone supposed to avoid it with all this **junk** lying around?« protested Jennifer.

junk: der Müll, der Unrat

»It's not junk. It's technology. But you wouldn't understand!« said Ben furiously.

Looking injured, Jennifer turned round. »Come on!« she told Miriam, and made **energetically** for the door

energetically: energisch

without bothering where she trod. This time a **light bulb**, two **electric switches** and a **plug** were crushed beneath her feet.

A minute later the girls were out in the street. *At last!* thought Ben, immediately sitting down at the computer again.

He sat in front of the screen for almost two hours without realizing how time was passing. Again and again he repeated the same manoeuvres: switch the computer off, switch the computer on again, wait for it to boot itself up, load the game, watch the game start, control the joystick, take the little figure into the shop where the magician ought to be. And then the error came up over and over again: the magician was nowhere in sight and the game froze.

After a while Ben began to feel hungry. He looked at his radio alarm. Just after six thirty.

That meant it was well past supper time. Funny that his mother wasn't home yet. She was never usually late for supper, and supper was at six **on the dot**, as Ben knew only too well. Because normally, at six on the dot, just about anywhere was a thousand times more interesting than his kitchen table at home. He might be at the swimming pool or on the football field, he might be in front of his computer or simply hanging around outside, but he always had to stop whatever he was doing just as he was enjoying himself, because they had supper at six. Ben's mother insisted.

light bulb: die Glühbirne
electric switch: der Elektroschalter
Plug: der Stecker

on the dot: punktgenau

Otherwise, Ben had to admit, he had a lot of freedom, he could talk to his mother about anything – or so she always said, anyway. But nothing would change her mind about supper. She wanted a quiet time with her only son at least once a day, she said. Ben didn't really understand that. Since his parents had **divorced** five years ago he visited his father on the other side of town only once a month, but he saw his mother every day. So why he always had to be home at six was one of the many things about grown-ups that **puzzled** him.

(to) divorce: sich scheiden lassen

(to) puzzle: verwirren, verblüffen

odd: merkwürdig, sonderbar

And now it was after six thirty. That was really **odd**. Even if something had happened to her – and nothing had ever happened to her before – Ben's mother would certainly have called him on her way home. Ben went into the kitchen and looked in the fridge. At least you could **rely** on that. Cold meat, cheese, butter, cola, there were even some sausages in the cool white refrigerator. Whatever day Ben looked in the fridge and at whatever time of day, there was always something to eat there. Ben helped himself to a **delicious** supper. Now perhaps his mother would finally see how well he could manage on his own, he thought. After all, he was nearly thirteen. But his mother sometimes seemed to think it was only his eighth birthday he'd be having in two weeks' time, if that.

(to) rely on sb/sth: sich auf jdn/etw verlassen

delicious: köstlich

Carrying three hot sausages and plenty of ketchup, two sandwiches with a double filling of sliced meat

and a chilled can of cola, Ben sat down at the kitchen table and looked out of the window. He could see almost the whole street from here. When his mother came back he'd be sure to spot her.
But nothing happened out in the street at all.
It wasn't just that Ben's mother didn't appear. There was nothing at all to be seen there. Or no human beings anyway. There was something very odd about that street. It had cars parked on both sides, same as usual. The shops – the bakery, the newsagent, the launderette, the little supermarket – had closed by now, of course. That was how it looked, anyway, but all the same Ben thought it was very strange to see no one at all out and about in the street. Not even a car driving down it.
That was it! At last Ben realized what was so odd. Not a single car driving along. That never happened! If there were no cars on the road something must be wrong somewhere. There's probably been a bad accident at the other end of the street, and the police had put up a **barrier**. Without hesitating for a moment, Ben flung on his shoes and jacket and raced out.
Soon he was at the road **junction** where he'd been so sure there must be an accident.
Nothing.
No accident, no police. Not a single car here either. Or rather, there *were* some cars in the middle of the road, but they were empty. Some of their engines

barrier: die Sperre, das Hindernis, die Straßensperre

junction: die Kreuzung

were still running, but there wasn't a soul in sight. Ben felt as if this was a ghost town. He stood at the junction all by himself, turned round several times, looked in all directions. What was going on? Who could he ask?

Jennifer! She'd been with him less than two hours ago. Then she'd been going to have an ice with Miriam. So if **something odd** had happened within the last two hours she'd be sure to have heard about it. Luckily Jennifer lived only two streets away.

something odd: etwas Merkwürdiges/Seltsames

Ben rang Jennifer's front door bell loud and long. The door was instantly flung open, and he found himself looking at Jennifer's surprised face. An expression of deep disappointment immediately came over it.

»What are you doing here?« sighed Jennifer. »I hoped it was my parents at last. I've been waiting over an hour for them. We were going to see a movie.«

»You mean *your* parents have disappeared, too?« asked Ben.

Briefly, he told Jennifer what had happened to him, and added, »What's up? Didn't you notice anything when you and Miriam went to have that ice?«

»We didn't have an ice after all,« Jennifer told him. »We were going to, yes, but there was no one serving in the café. We waited five minutes, and called out, but there was nobody there, so we went away again.«

Suddenly a number of wild ideas came into Ben's head: *For the first time ever my mother doesn't come home, there isn't a single car driving along the road, the city looks as if someone had* ***swept*** *the place clean, there's no one in the café and Jennifer's parents have gone too. It's . . .* »It's like in the computer game,« said Ben, finishing his **train of thought** out loud.

(to) sweep: fegen, kehren

train of thought: der Gedankengang

»Oh, for goodness' sake!« said Jennifer, irritated. »Can't you ever think of anything but your idiotic computer?«

»Sorry,« was all Ben muttered. Jennifer was right. How could he be thinking of his computer at a time like this? *But all the same, it really was like in his new computer game. More and more people keep disappearing from the city in the game as you move on, and it's always the grown-ups who go. The whole idea of the game is to get as many children as possible to join the figure and save the city. You score points for everything in town that you manage to keep functioning. That's how the game works – when it does work. But there was an error in the game. It had frozen. And now his mother had gone missing, and Jennifer was still waiting for her parents, and . . .*

»But that's **ridiculous**!« Once again Ben **uttered** his last thought out loud.

ridiculous: lächerlich, lachhaft
(to) utter: äußern

»What's ridiculous? Are you feeling okay?« Jennifer didn't know what to make of Ben. He stood there staring into space, muttering stuff that made no sense.

But Ben had come to a decision.

»Listen,« he told Jennifer. »You may think I'm crazy, but let's call all the others and ask what's going on round at their places.«

»All what others?« Jennifer was lost.

»Well, our friends,« said Ben. »Frank, Miriam, Thomas and so on.«

Jennifer didn't think much of that idea. How could Miriam, for instance, have anything to do with her parents not coming home? But Ben seemed so sure of what he was doing that she didn't **object**. She found the little pink phone book where she kept all her girlfriends' numbers, got down on the floor by the phone with Ben, and they began calling number after number in turn. Quarter of an hour later Ben was sure.

(to) object: protestieren, einwenden

»Miriam's still waiting for her parents too. Thomas is staying with his grandmother at the moment and she's suddenly disappeared. And Frank's big brother who's supposed to be keeping an eye on the apartment while his Dad's away on a business trip hasn't turned up yet. I don't know how it happened, but I'm sure now. Anyone older than fifteen has vanished!«

»What makes you say fifteen?« asked Jennifer. »Are you finally going to tell me just what this mysterious puzzle you're trying to solve is?«

Ben told her the rules of his computer game.

»Don't you see?« he went on. »In the computer game everyone older than fifteen disappears. And that's exactly what's happened here in this city!«

»You mean your computer game has turned real?«

»It may sound crazy but yes, that's exactly what I mean.«

»You'**re round the twist**!«

(to) be round the twist: verrückt sein

»Then tell me where Miriam's and Thomas' and Frank's parents and grandmother and older brothers and sisters have gone.«

»But it can't be true!« cried Jennifer. Her voice was trembling. **Goosebumps** slowly crawled up her arms. Her eyes were **damp**, and she felt like crying, but she managed to keep back the tears. No, she wouldn't cry, not until she was perfectly sure about Ben's **daft** theory.

»Come on!« she told Ben. »I want to see if what you're saying is right.«

goosebumps: die Gänsehaut
damp: feucht

daft: blöd, bekloppt

Now what?

Jennifer **hauled** Ben back to the telephone.

»What's the idea?« he asked.

»If you're right there oughtn't to be any grown-ups around at all,« said Jennifer. »So now I'm going to call all the grown-ups I know: my grandparents and aunts and uncles, my parents' numbers at work and so on. And you'll do exactly the same, Ben!«

»Not a bad idea,« Ben agreed. So they called number after number, but no one ever picked up the phone. After the seventeenth call they finally stopped for a break.

»I'm afraid I was right,« said Ben. »Now what?«

»Now what?« cried Jennifer. »How would I know? It's *your* **wretched** computer game!«

(to) haul: schleppen, ziehen

wretched: elend, erbärmlich, hier im Sinne von: verdammt

»You're saying it's because of my computer game no one's around any more? What makes you think so? I only said it's just like on the computer. That doesn't mean my game is the reason. How do you think a thing like that would happen? I mean, it's nonsense!«

»I've no idea how it happened. All I know is everything was okay until you started playing that stupid game,« Jennifer **snapped** back.

Ben felt a large **lump** in his throat – a lump made up of fury and anxiety combined. It wasn't his fault all the grown-ups were missing, after all! Or was it? *I was only playing the game*, thought Ben. *I did everything the right way, but then the game itself went wrong. I can't help it. And technically it just isn't possible for a computer game to make adults disappear. But suppose it did? Is it really my fault we're on our own?* It was Ben who had tears in his eyes now. »I just don't understand any of this,« he **gulped**.

Jennifer immediately felt **pity**.

»Sorry,« she whispered. »I didn't mean to shout at you like that. But I'**m scared**. I mean, what are we going to do?«

»I'm scared, too,« said Ben. He thought how this very morning he'd been cross that his mother didn't take him seriously, she always treated him like a little boy, he was a lot older than she thought. But now that Ben thought of his mother being gone, and how maybe there weren't any adults at all left in town, he

(to) snap: blaffen, schnauzen
lump: der Kloß, der Klumpen

(to) gulp: würgen, schlucken, hier: schluchzen
pity: das Mitleid

(to) be scared: Angst haben

suddenly didn't feel as grown up. Far from it. Right now he felt very small and helpless.

»Maybe,« he said, **dashing** a tear out of his left eye, »maybe we ought to get together with Miriam and Frank and tell them about all this. They might think of something.«

Half an hour later all four of them **were round** at Jennifer's. Ben and Jennifer, both of them still **upset**, had **laboriously** explained everything to their friends. Miriam and Frank, naturally enough, didn't believe a word of it, so they decided to have a good look around the neighbourhood.

The four children went out into the street. There were still cars parked everywhere. None of them were moving. On the opposite side of the street there was a pizzeria. Frank knew it stayed open till late at night. He went across and looked in. No one in sight, but black smoke was **billowing out** of the pizza oven. Frank looked around, went in, grabbed the nearest towel, wrapped it round his hand and opened the oven, to be met by a thick, greasy, black cloud of fumes. Frank jumped backwards, waved his arms around to get some air and coughed.

»**Burnt to a cinder**,« said Miriam, looking at the pizza in the stove, or rather what was left of the pizza. It was now nothing but a **charred**, hard, black disk, still **smouldering**. Miriam turned the oven off.

»A few minutes more and the whole place would have gone up in flames,« said Jennifer. Ben looked

(to) dash: wischen

(to) be round: versammelt sein, zusammensitzen
upset: aufgeregt, aufgebracht
laboriously: umständlich, mühsam

(to) billow out: (in Schwaden) hervorquellen

burnt to a cinder: völlig verkohlt

charred: verkohlt

(to) smoulder: schwelen, schmoren

around him. Half-eaten pizzas lay on the tables, with half-empty glasses beside them. There was even money still lying on some of the tables, too.

(to) magic (-ck): (ver-)zaubern

»Looks like someone suddenly **magicked** everyone away,« he said. The children looked at each other in horror.

»Come on, let's look next door,« suggested Miriam.

All four of them made for the hairdresser's next to the pizzeria. Hot water was running from the tap in one of the basins. Cut hair lay about on the floor. Gel was **oozing out** of an open tube on a little table. At the chair next to it a **razor** lay on the floor buzzing quietly to itself. You could tell from the sound that the battery wouldn't last much longer. A hairdryer kept blowing hot air into the empty room – because there wasn't a soul here either.

(to) ooze out: herausquellen
razor: der Rasierapparat

»Just like in the pizzeria,« said Miriam.

»Yes,« agreed Ben. »What did I tell you? All the grown-ups have disappeared.«

Frank **clutched** his head in both hands and **groaned**. »But this is crazy! No one's going to believe us!«

(to) clutch: umklammern
(to) groan: stöhnen

»Don't let that bother you,« said Miriam dryly. »You won't have to tell anyone; the kids will notice it for themselves and the grown-ups are gone anyway.«

»That's right,« said Ben. »And that's the **approach** we'd better take – I mean, we don't want to tell anyone for now, not until we know more about how it happened, and most important of all how we can put things right again.«

approach: der Ansatz, die Einstellung

»Yes, that's the thing to do,« Frank agreed with his friend. »Let's swear to keep it secret. And we'll all discuss any step we take together before telling anyone else about it.«

»Oh, why not found a secret society and be done with it?« said Miriam **caustically**. »Then we can **embroider** ourselves **badges** and elect you chairman. You boys are sometimes **weird**! I'm not doing anything at all for now. Maybe everything will be okay again tomorrow. Till then I'm just going to think of something else.«

Jennifer agreed. »Let's all go back to my place,« she suggested. »I don't know what else might happen tonight, but I do know I don't want to be alone.«

She said what everyone else was thinking. They went back to Jennifer's together.

In Jennifer's parents' living room Miriam immediately switched the TV set on. But the screen was blank.

»Very clever,« said Ben sarcastically. »Who did you think puts the TV programmes out on the air? Dear little **brownies** doing the job when the grown-ups go missing?«

Miriam **spun** around furiously and was about to make for Ben. Jennifer knew that angry expression on her friend's face. It usually meant trouble – big trouble. She quickly barred Miriam's way. »Don't you two have anything better to do right now than fight? If you ask me, those are both good suggestions."

»Both?« asked Frank.

caustically: bissig, schnippisch
(to) embroider: sticken
badge: das Abzeichen
weird: seltsam

brownie: das Heinzelmännchen

(to) spin: drehen

»That's right,« said Jennifer. »For now, we won't mention Ben's computer game to anyone, and we'll discuss everything we do with each other. But first let's wait till tomorrow morning and find out what's really going on in the city.«

»And let's go to school, too, first thing tomorrow,« suggested Miriam.

blankly: verständnislos

Ben looked at her **blankly**.

»There won't be any lessons,« she went on, »but you always find out what's going on at school first.«

The others could see the point of that, so between them the four children decided to go to school at the usual time next day.

Miriam turned out to be right: when they reached school in the morning the yard was full of children talking excitedly about what had happened the evening before. Well, so they all knew about it, even if no one could explain where the grown-ups were and when they'd be back. Ben suddenly had an idea. He **clambered up** a **drainpipe** to the roof of one of the **school sheds** and shouted: »Everyone listen!« When he had yelled this five times the noise in the school yard actually did die down a little. To the astonishment of his three friends, Ben began making a speech.

(to) clamber up: hinaufklettern
drainpipe: die Regenrinne, das Abflussrohr
school shed: *hier:* der Schulpavillon

»You all know what's happened,« he shouted at the top of his voice. Not many of them could hear what he was saying, but Ben didn't let that bother him. He just went on yelling:

»All the grown-ups have gone. Since we don't know when they'll be back we have to decide what we're going to do. Anyone who wants to join meets in ten minutes' time in the school hall, so we can . . .« But Ben got no further. Yells and shouts **drowned him out**.
»Mummy's boy!« shouted some of the kids who felt they were **particularly** big and strong. »Can't manage without your mum?« Of course there were plenty of people ready to laugh at this.
»Hey, why don't we paint the town red?« suggested another boy.
»That's right!« – shouted a third. »If we can be sure the adults have gone, know what I'm going to do?« The kids standing around stared at him expectantly. Did someone have a good idea? The loud-mouthed boy **relished** the effect of his pause. Then he took a deep breath and shouted: »I'm going into town **to grab** anything I want from the shops. For free! Because there's no one left to ask for money!«
And that was it, where Ben's speech was concerned. A **deafening** shout of **glee** echoed around the school yard. Suddenly, panic broke out as if the school were burning down. Hundreds of pupils rushed to the gates, all of them wanting to be the first to reach town.
»No, don't!« shouted Ben at the top of his voice, but no one was listening. A huge torrent of kids was pouring across the road in the direction of the city centre. Some of them waited a moment, **snatched**

(to) drown sb out: jdn niederschreien, übertönen

particularly: besonders

(to) relish: genießen, auskosten
(to) grab: grabschen

deafening: ohrenbetäubend
glee: die Freude

(to) snatch: greifen, grabschen

up a few stones from the ground and flung them at the classroom windows. Ben put his hands over his ears. There were tears in his eyes. All around him was the clink of breaking glass and the yells of his fellow pupils as they threw a few more stones, laughing, and then raced after the wildly excited crowd making off **to loot** the shops. Ben sat on the roof of the shed crying quietly, and taking one last look across the yard.

(to) loot: plündern

Miriam, Jennifer, and Frank were leaning on the school wall side by side, eyes still wide and mouths still open. They didn't say a word. About twenty children were still **hovering** between them and Ben, talking to each other, walking round in circles, shifting from foot to foot. They were in complete **confusion** and didn't know what to do. Their eyes were reddened – they'd probably been crying half the night because their parents hadn't come home. They'd hoped to find some explanation of what had happened here at school, so they'd been glad of Ben's idea of a meeting in the school hall. But then the others all ran off, and now they didn't know what to do.

(to) hover: herumstehen

confusion: das Durcheinander, der Wirrwarr

Ben climbed down from the roof. Frank raced towards him, shouting furiously: »Oh, great! Absolutely brilliant! I thought we were going to discuss every step we took first! But of course you had **to shoot your mouth off** – and now look what you've done. What do you think's going on in town now?«

(to) shoot one´s mouth off: das Maul aufreißen

Jennifer and Miriam had joined him.
»Oh, come off it, Frank,« said Jennifer. »You think anyone could have stopped them going off like that? I saw a movie once something like this. There was a sinking ship, but instead of stopping to think how to save themselves most of the passengers panicked and did all kinds of stupid things.«
»That's right,« Miriam agreed. »I saw that movie too. There was this really great scene when . . .«
Frank cut Miriam short. »That's hardly helpful at this moment, Miriam!« he said angrily.
Miriam fell silent. Jennifer went on trying to make the peace. »Your idea of a meeting was a good one, Ben, but it really would have been better to tell us your plan first.«
»Well, the idea of the meeting came to me so suddenly,« Ben said, his voice shaking, »I just didn't have time to think of discussing it with you. Anyway, if I'd thought of it ahead I wouldn't have dared make a speech. It just kind of came over me.«
»That's okay,« Jennifer said **soothingly**. Frank was still muttering crossly to himself.

soothingly: beruhigend, beschwichtigend

Miriam was baffled. »But what's so bad about going into town?« she asked the others. »To be honest, I've always dreamed of going crazy in a big store. And now the grown-ups aren't around we can do it. I mean, we can take this opportunity, right?«
»Oh, for goodness' sake, Miriam!« Frank exploded. First Ben striking out on his own and wrecking any

chance that they could all help each other, and now here was Miriam obviously unable to understand their real situation. It was more than he could take. Red in the face, he was about **to give her a piece of his mind,** but Jennifer stepped in. »Let's not start quarrelling again,« she said quickly. »Why don't we go into town and see what's going on? Then Miriam will understand what we mean, too.«

(to) give sb a piece of one's mind: jdm eine Standpauke halten

»Then Miriam will understand what we mean, too!« said Miriam, mimicking her friend. »Don't act so smart just because I ask a question. I'll bet the rest of you've sometimes dreamed of being able to run wild in a department store, only you don't want to admit it.«

But before another quarrel could start up, someone else suddenly spoke behind them.

»What's up now?« The four friends turned around. There was Thomas. He was one of the twenty or so children who hadn't chased off to the city centre.

»I thought we were going to discuss what to do next?« Thomas added, as if nothing had happened in the school yard.

»Listen!« said Jennifer, who felt like getting something done instead of just standing around talking. »Let's all meet outside the school hall at four this afternoon. Tell anyone else who wants to come! Until then we can all take a look around town. We'll **pool** all our information this afternoon and think what to do. Okay? Off we go, then!«

(to) pool: zusammentragen, vereinen

And Jennifer had turned and was marching firmly down the street. Ben and Frank stood there staring at her in surprise. Miriam was grinning.
»Madam Chairwoman has spoken! Well, are we going or do you plan to stand here until you **take root**?« So saying, she took an arm of both boys and started off after Jennifer, pulling them along with her. Thomas called out, »Okay, I'll be there at four.« But the others were some way off already.

(to) take root: Wurzeln schlagen

Chaos Breaks Out

Ben had seen many **battlefields**, he'd mixed with tough characters and daring **crooks** – but in his computer games. He had never dreamed of having to face anything like that in real life. Now he was right in the middle of the battle. And not in some way-out adventure game full of mystic **enchanted forests** or mysterious UFO landing sites, but in the ordinary **surroundings** of the shopping centre in his home town, only twenty minutes from his comfortable home.
The floor of the shopping mall was covered with splinters of glass from broken **display windows**. Dummies hung out of the windows with their arms or legs chopped off. Cream tarts were sticking to the walls, and many of the doors were so covered with ketchup you'd have thought someone was shooting

battlefield: das Schlachtfeld
crook : der Gauner

enchanted forest: der Zauberwald

surrounding: die Umgebung

display window: das Schaufenster

a spaghetti Western here. In the greengrocer's, about thirty boys were busy **staging an attack** on the **fishmonger's**, throwing eggs, tomatoes, peaches and melons. Their **opponents**, entrenched behind tubs of **pickled gherkins**, were replying to this offensive with a **volley** of **mackerel** and salted sardines. Several girls in **velvet** evening dresses, red, blue, or glittering with gold **sequins**, were moving across the battlefield in high-heeled shoes, **squealing**. They were just in time to leap out of the way as a horde of boys in black leathers on brand-new mopeds **thundered past** them towards the café, where about thirty boys were having a cream-cake fight with twenty girls. A crowd of children were **dragging** hi-fi systems **by the crateful** out of the electronics store and through the mall, accompanied by hundreds of flying CDs being used by a small group of bigger boys as frisbees. But the CDs were nothing like such dangerous weapons as the hard balls being fired out of the sports centre where some of the kids had fixed up a baseball field. Ben might have found it easier to avoid them if their **orbits** hadn't kept crossing with the wooden arrows whistling through the shopping mall above their heads. A few idiots were playing Robin Hood with bows and arrows.

»They're crazy!« shouted Frank. Even before Ben could turn to him, he had raced into the sports centre. As he ran he snatched up a golf club and made for the **archers**.

(to) stage an attack: einen Angriff durchführen
fishmonger's: der Fischladen
opponent: der Gegner
pickled gherkins: die Gewürzgurken
volley: die Salve
mackerel: die Makrele
velvet: der Samt
sequin: die Paillette
(to) squeal: schreien, kreischen
(to) thunder past: vorbeidonnern
(to) drag: schleppen
by the crateful: kistenweise
orbit: die Flugbahn
archer: der Bogenschütze

»You total idiots!« he yelled, swinging the club wildly around him. »Put those bows and arrows down or **I'll knock** you **into the middle of next week.** Do you want to murder us or what?«

to knock into the middle of next week: in Grund und Boden hauen

Most of the archers immediately dropped their weapons in alarm and **made for cover**. But three of them just grinned at Frank and put new arrows to their bows.

(to) make for cover: Schutz suchen

»Stay at home if you're scared! You can't boss us around, anyway. We can do as we like,« said one of them. His name was Kolya.

Kolya was one school class above Frank, who was in Class Seven along with Ben, Jennifer and Miriam, but Frank knew the older boy well. If there was a fight anywhere in the school yard you could bet Kolya would be involved. And quite often it was Frank that Kolya was fighting. Kolya never missed a chance **to bully** other children, steal from them or even threaten violence if they didn't do things for him: do his homework, buy him sweets or liquor from the store near school – with their own money, of course. No one dared stand up to Kolya. He'd shown how strong he was only too often by beating up another boy in public.

(to) bully: schikanieren, tyrannisieren

Frank was the only boy who wasn't afraid of him. And he didn't need to fear Kolya either, because he, Frank, was not just the keenest but also the most talented athlete in the school. Frank spent every moment of his leisure time on sports: he went to karate training on Mondays and Wednesdays, he did athletics on Tuesdays, he spent Thursday afternoon at the swimming club, Friday was for rowing, and he always had a match or sporting competition of some kind at the weekends.

Now he was standing with his golf club raised in front of Kolya, who was about to send another arrow winging its way right through the shopping centre. But even before he had bent the bow, Kolya heard something whistle briefly through the air. He felt the wood vibrate as it cracked in his hand, and looked in surprise at the shattered bow. Frank had struck a well-aimed blow and broken it in half. The other two archers now **meekly** put their bows down, **retreated** a couple of steps and looked at Kolya and Frank, who were facing each other with grim expressions. Kolya's face **distorted** again into a **supercilious** grin.

meekly: widerstandslos, hier: brav
(to) retreat: sich zurückziehen

(to) distort: verzerren
supercilious: hochnäsig
(to) mock: spotten, frotzeln

»Well, little Mister Cop?« he **mocked**. »Going to keep me in line, are you? Have fun! I have plenty more ideas.«

He called to his friends, laughing and waving his hand, and ran out of the store with the other boys in tow. Meanwhile Ben, Jennifer and Miriam had reached the sports centre too. They had been watching the whole show in suspense. Frank turned to Miriam.

»That's why I was against it back in the school yard – against the idea of helping ourselves from stores, I mean. I've had fights with Kolya often enough; I knew he'd be bound to give us even more trouble than he usually does in school.«

»Yes, I see that too now,« sighed Miriam. »And anyway, everything's quite different from how I always imagined. I just thought it'd be terrific to be in a store where you could take anything you liked. All those lovely toys, the nice clothes, all the stuff you put on your wish list at Christmas and birthdays, and you could have it all at once. You'd only have to reach out and get it. And plenty for everyone – at least if you don't **chuck** half of it out of the window and **wreck** it.«

(to) chuck: schmeißen
(to) wreck: zerstören

»Exactly – and look at this, I mean, everyone going crazy and grabbing whatever they can get hold of, as if the grown-ups would be back any moment and stop it,« added Jennifer.

»I just wish they *would*,« gulped Miriam. »I'd rather that than my silly dream. But – but who knows if our parents will ever be back?«

Ben, Jennifer and Frank went white in the face. They looked at each other in silence.

»That's right, who *does* know if they'll ever be back at all?« said Ben at last, echoing Miriam.

Frank had seen Ben's point at once. »Which means we might have to survive on our own for quite some time. And right now there are kids having fights with food, chucking it round the place.«

At that very moment, as if to back up what Frank said, a large squashy tomato hit the back of Ben's head. It was a shot **deflected** from the vegetable ver-

(to) deflect: ablenken, abfälschen

venue: der Austragungsort, der Treffpunkt

sus seafood fight, which had briefly shifted its **venue** to the sports shop.

»We'll have to do something,« snapped Ben, mopping the back of his head with a tennis shirt. The tennis shirt had quite an expensive price ticket on it. »Hey, come into the big department store with me. I have an idea.«

cul-de-sac: die Sackgasse

(to) plunge: eintauchen

(to) gobble up: schlucken, verschlucken

rack: der Ständer, das Gestell

glaring: grell

At the far end of the shopping mall with all its separate shops on both sides there was a large department store on four floors, turning the mall into a **cul-de-sac**. Once you reached the store, you could only turn back or **plunge** into its open jaws, which were just waiting **to gobble up** your money. After wandering along countless narrow aisles between **racks** of clothes and stands of other assorted goods, along mini-mazes lined with mirrors and loud video shows, past perfumed salesgirls and **glaring** Special Offer notices, you usually ended up reaching what looked like an exit but wasn't, without a penny in your pocket. At least, that had happened to Ben only too often once he stepped inside the department store.

looted: geplündert

But everything was different now. There were no perfumed salesgirls around, the video screens were blank and silent, most of the mirrors were splinters of glass lying on the floor, the racks of clothing had been tipped over or **looted** and were empty, the mountains of assorted goods were scattered all over the place, and the escalators had been turned into test drives for mountain bikes.

»We'd better look for the office,« Ben told his friends.
»What office?« asked Frank.
»Well, every big store has an office somewhere. For the admin and so on,« said Ben. »And I bet you the keys to the stockrooms are in that office. I mean, what you see here in the main store is just a display for the customers, and when something's sold out it has to be restocked. Which means there should be more of everything here still sitting in packing cases in the **stockrooms**. If we're in luck no one else has thought of that yet, so at least we can see what's still available. Specially food.«

stockroom: der Lagerraum, die Lagerhalle

»That's a really good idea,« agreed Miriam. »And I know where the office is, too.«
»You do?« said the surprised Jennifer.
»Yup,« admitted Miriam. »Well, it's like this – some stupid store detective picked me up once just because I **nicked** a stuffed toy duck for my little brother. So they took me off to the office and then . . .«.

(to) nick: mitgehen lassen, klauen

But here Miriam stopped short in mid-sentence. She suddenly went quite pale around the nostrils and struck her forehead with the palm of her hand. »Oh, my God!« she cried.
»Miriam, what's the matter?« asked Jennifer, sounding worried.
»My brother!« said Miriam. »I forgot about my brother!«
»You have a brother?« asked Frank, surprised.
»My little brother Mike. He's three years old,« Miriam

nursery: der Kindergarten, der Hort

explained. »He goes to **nursery**. My parents always fetch him when they finish work and bring him home with them. But they didn't come home at all yesterday evening. And I forgot my brother!«

»Oh no!« cried Jennifer. »We'll have to go to the nursery this minute! Goodness knows how many little kids are still in there! You can bet all the nursery staff vanished yesterday too.«

»Look, you two girls go to the nursery,« Ben told Jennifer and Miriam. »Frank and I will see what we can find in the way of stockrooms. Let's all of us meet in the school hall around four.«

Jennifer and Miriam ran off to the sports department of the big store, where they found two racing bikes and pedalled off to the nursery on them. Frank and Ben set off for the office, after Miriam had told them the way. *What else is going to happen?* Ben wondered. *Oh well, no time to think about that now. First things first, and that means the stockrooms. We'll think about the rest this afternoon. I hope.*

More Unwelcome Surprises

(to) bawl: brüllen, schreien

Miriam and Jennifer were prepared for the worst. They hurtled along the empty streets on the racing bikes, imagining the horrors of the scene in the nursery. In her mind's eye, Miriam saw her little brother standing at the window **bawling**, miserable because he'd been forgotten. And the other little kids would be **milling around** in just the same state. They'd hear the pitiful wailing of the abandoned children quite a long way off, thought Miriam. Mingled tears and sweat ran down her face as she **summoned up** all her strength to push the pedals down even harder. She had never ridden a bike so fast before, let alone a racing bike she didn't know at all.

Jennifer had a sinking feeling in her stomach, too. Not because of the pace Miriam was setting on the racing bike; she could easily keep up. She'd always been more athletic than her friend, and now she was cycling along close behind Miriam without any difficulty. But she too was picturing the dreadful scene ahead of them: babies and toddlers howling and weeping, waiting for help. And exactly what were they going to do once they reached the nursery? They couldn't possibly leave the little kids on their own. Someone had to look after them, but how? They themselves couldn't take all those children home! And another, even worse thought was that by no means all the small children in town went to nursery. What about all the babies and toddlers home alone at this minute? How were they going to help them? How were they even going to find them in the first place? Who knew for certain which families had small children? The more Jennifer thought about it the worse she felt. All the same, she went on cycling. They must get there first, and then sort it all out somehow or other.

(to) mill around: umherlaufen, hier: herumwuseln

(to) summon up: zusammenraffen, aufbringen, aufbieten

The nursery was already in sight. They couldn't hear the miserable, wailing kids yet. Only another few metres. Miriam and Jennifer braked sharply. Their back wheels slipped, and both girls braced their feet on the road so as not to lose their balance. Then they stood there looking **incredulously** at each other. All was quiet. Too quiet. What had happened? How come they couldn't hear anything? Slowly, the girls got off their bikes and leaned them against the wall of the building. They waited for a moment, listening: nothing! There wasn't a sound to be heard.

incredulously: ungläubig, skeptisch, zweifelnd

»Mike?« called Miriam, her voice shaking. Jennifer didn't like this at all. *My God, what's happened here?* she thought, but she dared not say it aloud. She didn't want to **scare** her best friend even more.

(to) scare: erschrecken

»Mike, where are you?« cried Miriam, her voice firmer this time. Soon she was shouting. Jennifer joined in.

»Mike! Mi-ike!« yelled both girls as loud as they could. But nothing **stirred**.

(to) stir: sich rühren

Jennifer turned and carefully examined their surroundings. Not a child in sight. The old swing hung there in the empty playground in front of the main building, squealing slightly. Buckets, plastic spades, toy cars and even a pale blue anorak lay all **jumbled up** in the sandbox. Whoever had been playing there had left the sandbox in a hurry, and no one had bothered to clear up. A similar picture presented itself to Jennifer on the little playing field. A few balls were ly-

jumbled up: durcheinander, kunterbunt vermischt

ing about on the grass, along with a **scooter** that had fallen over and a few half-eaten sandwiches. But no children.

scooter: der Tretroller

»Jennifer!« called a voice from the building. Miriam put her head out of a first-floor window. »I've looked everywhere. Nothing! Do you understand? There's no one here! The whole place is empty! Where's my brother? Where have they all gone? Jennifer, what am I going to do now?«

Jennifer thought she'd better see this for herself. She knew it was silly, really. Miriam would have been sure to search everywhere, but all the same Jennifer wanted to take a look, too.

And of course Miriam was right. The corridors, all the rooms, the kitchen, even the toilets – there wasn't a child to be found.

»Just like outside,« said Jennifer finally, going back to Miriam. »They've all gone!«

»Now what?« **sobbed** Miriam, with tears in her eyes. She'd forgotten all about her little brother and now he'd disappeared. How could she ever forgive herself? Who knew where he might be at this moment, hopelessly lost and crying his eyes out?

(to) sob: schluchzen

»We'll have to search the whole city,« said Miriam. »I just have to find my brother.«

Jennifer agreed. They couldn't **leave** the poor kid **in the lurch**. »I know where to start,« she said. »Let's go to the hospital.«

(to) leave sb in the lurch: jdn im Stich lassen, jdn hängen lassen

»Why the hospital?« Miriam was baffled. She could

imagine finding her little brother in all sorts of places: on lonely streets, in empty shops, maybe in the park or somewhere like that, but surely not at the hospital.

»Well, look,« explained Jennifer, »we don't really know anything much so far. It looks like all the grown-ups have disappeared, and there's chaos in the shopping centre. That's all we're sure of. But whatever's happened it's an emergency, some kind of disaster. And where does everyone go when there's a disaster? To the hospital! I want to find your kid brother, but I want to find out just what's going on, too, so let's go!«

Miriam could see the sense of that, but she wouldn't have had a chance to contradict her friend anyway. Jennifer was already on the way back to her bike. So Miriam ran after her, and they both set off for the hospital.

Meanwhile Ben and Frank had found the key to the stockrooms, and they soon located the stockrooms themselves. Every department store was built on the same principle, after all. Trucks of goods must have direct access to the stockroom area, so the two boys had only to go out in the street and look for a place where trucks could drive up and **unload**.

(to) unload: entladen
(to) fit: passen

The key **fitted**, and it was easy to open the big gate of the stockrooms. Ben and Frank stood in the first one surrounded by huge shelves.

»This lot must be four metres high,« said Frank in **amazement**. Nothing but shelves as far as they could see, stacked high with countless brown cartons.

amazement: das Erstaunen, die Verwunderung

»Now we have to search,« said Ben. »Which of those cartons might have food in them? Isn't there a cold store anywhere for the **perishable** stuff?«

perishable: verderblich

»This place is big enough to drive you crazy,« said Frank. »We'd better search separately. Let's meet again here in half an hour.«

Good idea, Ben thought. He said he would go left and Frank could go right.

It seemed the long corridor with the stockrooms off it would never end. *Must be a hundred or a hundred and fifty metres long*, thought Ben. And that was only half the width of the whole area. Frank was searching the other half. Every three metres another corridor branched straight off the main one. Each of them was probably a good fifty metres long, too. But there was no door or passage anywhere that looked as if it led to a cold store. Just more and more shelves stacked with endless numbers of brown cartons bearing little white stickers and sets of numbers.

Ben would never have thought stockrooms containing all the wonderful things he'd ever wished for could look so boring. There he was in the middle of the things on his Christmas and birthday wish lists, just looking for something to eat – and there was no food in sight.

»**Drat it all!**« **cursed** Ben to himself. *There just had to*

drat it all!: Verflixt!
(to) curse: fluchen, verfluchen

cold store: das Kühlhaus

be a **cold store** *somewhere in these stockrooms. Where else would they keep all the sausages, the meat, the cheese, the milk?* Wherever Ben looked, he saw nothing but a blank grey wall at the far end of every corridor. A wall so massive and forbidding that it seemed useless even to start in that direction. *No point in it*, thought Ben. Angrily, he kicked one of the cartons stored on a bottom shelf. In fact he kicked it so hard that he made a hole in the carton, and some white, powdery stuff trickled out. Ben bent down to take a closer look. He caught some of the powder in one hand and rubbed it between the thumb and forefinger of the other. *Wait a minute, I know this. It's . . . it's . . .* Suddenly he knew what it was – and something much worse occurred to him, too. He put his hand into the left-hand pocket of his jeans, where he always kept the splendid Swiss knife his father had given him last Christmas. Two quick cuts, and the carton was gaping open. »Oh, hell!« cursed Ben. He turned on his heel and sprinted back to the meeting place agreed with Frank.

»Frank! Fraaank!« shouted Ben as he ran. »Fraaank! You can stop looking. There's no point in it.«

»No point in what?« Frank put his head around the corner of the third corridor. Ben had already reached him.

»Looking for the cold store,« said Ben, annoyed with himself. »How could we be so stupid?« There was no calming him down.

»What do you mean? Why are we stupid?« Frank was baffled.
»Because we are, that's why,« Ben went on furiously. »What do you think I've just found?«
»The cold store?« suggested Frank, thinking that was the most likely thing. Ben just snorted.
»Packets of **instant potato**!«
»So?«
»Instant potato – you know, it looks like white powder, and you use it to make instant mash or potato pancakes!«
»Yum,« said Frank, smacking his lips **with relish**.
Ben pulled himself together as best he could, and **refrained** from grabbing Frank by the throat. He took three deep breaths and then said, »Frank, have you ever bought any meat in this store? Or fresh milk?«
»Nope. My mum and dad do the shopping.«
Ben fought for air. »There *isn't* any fresh meat in this store!« he shouted. »And no fresh milk and no fresh sausage, not even fresh vegetables. There's only canned and instant stuff. That's why they don't have any cold store.«
Before Frank could say anything, Ben went on: »The only shops with fresh food in this whole shopping centre are the smaller ones in the mall – the fishmonger's, the cheese shop, the greengrocer's and so forth. They're not big enough to need a large cold store. All their stuff is in the chilled cabinets and freezers they have in the shop itself. And right now

instant potato: das Kartoffelpüreepulver

with relish: genüsslich
(to) refrain: absehen von, unterlassen

there's about a hundred or two hundred kids out there among those chilled cabinets and freezers, with nothing better to do than throw the food at each other. The last and only fresh food anywhere in this shopping centre. So here we are surrounded by cans and packets looking for a cold store. That's why we were stupid!«

Ben was so furious that his voice broke. He thought of the fridge at home that was always full, he thought of his mother making breakfast every morning. He even thought of supper at six on the dot. How happily he'd drop whatever he was doing to be home just when his mum said and let her give him a delicious hot supper! Instead, here he was in a huge department store's stockrooms looking for fresh food that wasn't there. Tears rolled down Ben's face, his hands trembled, he was red in the face and his throat felt swollen. By now Frank, too, had **grasped** the situation, but he felt helpless and didn't know what to say. So he just put an arm around his friend Ben and cursed quietly to himself.

(to) **grasp**: begreifen

The Meeting

Frank and Ben were outside the main school hall punctually at four. They were the only people there. More from habit than anything, Frank tried the door. »How come it's open?« he said in surprise. The answer promptly came from inside. Thomas was standing there. He had been just about to look out and see if Ben and his friends had arrived yet.

»I unlocked it,« said Thomas proudly. »One of the cleaning ladies dropped her keys in the corridor once, understand? So of course I wasn't going to leave all those keys there. Because if you find something lying about and you're a collector the main thing is . . .«

». . .that it's for free and you only have to pick it up,« Ben finished Thomas's famous **maxim**. »Are you telling us,« he added, »you have all the keys to this school building?«

maxim: die Maxime

»That's right,« Thomas confirmed, feeling that his passion for collecting things might yet come in very useful.

»Good, excellent,« muttered Ben.

»Who else has turned up for the meeting ?« Frank was remembering what they'd come for.

»There's twelve people here so far,« said Thomas. »With you that's fourteen. But a few more were going to come. Weren't Jennifer and Miriam planning to be back, too?«

»You mean they're not here yet?« Ben was surprised. He hurried into the hall to see for himself. There were twelve children excitedly exchanging news of what they'd seen that morning. Sure enough, Jennifer and Miriam weren't among them. Ben nervously ran a hand through his hair. A horrible thought came into his head. *I hope to goodness they haven't disappeared, too.* Without the two girls they'd be in real trouble. It was hard enough for him anyway, working out the general situation, wondering what to do, keeping calm and dealing with the **constant** fear that they'd never manage to survive in this city on their own. But if two of his three best friends were missing as well, that would be terrible. Ben shook off the **dreadful** idea quickly.

constant: ständig, andauernd

dreadful: furchtbar, schrecklich

»Okay,« he began at once, more to take his mind off the girls than anything else, but also because someone had to do something. »Let's start right away. I suggest we all say in turn what we've found out. Then we can think what to do next.«

No one had actually chosen Ben as chairman of the meeting, but they were all too anxious to know what was going on to bother about that. They agreed with Ben that they'd better start the meeting at once.

»Well, no TV sets are working,« began a boy Ben didn't know. He must be from one of the lower classes. Ben guessed he was eight or at the most nine. »I've been trying all day, every channel and on lots of different sets, but the screen's always blank.«

»Yes, we know. There's nobody left around **to transmit** programmes,« Frank interrupted the little boy. The child shut his mouth, injured. So he'd been spending all day sitting in front of TV sets, trying to find out something that all the others knew already, and they thought it was perfectly natural! Somebody

(to) transmit: übertragen, übermitteln

might have told him, thought the little boy. But the others took no notice of him.

»So what else is *new*?« asked Ben, a touch impatiently.

»My horses are still there!« said Kathrin happily. She was twelve and in the parallel class to Ben. »I **groomed** them and fed them, but I'll soon be needing more **oats** for them. Anyone know where I can get oats?« She looked expectantly round. No one had the faintest idea.

(to) groom: striegeln
oats (*pl*): der Hafer

Frank looked meaningfully at Ben. *Animals! That's another thing. As if we didn't have enough problems already. Who was going to look after the animals now? How many were there in town anyway? What living creatures would be around, other than horses, dogs and cats?*

Although Frank hadn't said a word, Ben understood his look. »Did you just feed and groom your horses or did you see any other animals?« he asked Kathrin.

»Other animals? No, I just went to see my horses. I mean, I had to look after them. I thought if the grown-ups are gone then the man at the livery stable would be gone, too. And he was,« said Kathrin.

»My dog's at home!« interrupted a boy called Philip. That **set the ball rolling**.

(to) set the ball rolling: den Stein ins Rollen bringen, den Anfang machen, hier: eine Lawine lostreten

»I have a budgie at home. He's there, too,« said another boy.

»So are my two cats. They're fine.«

»I have a dog, he's *that* big and he always . . .«

»Yes, yes, okay!« Frank tried to calm the meeting.

»Obviously you all have pets at home – except Ben and me.«

»I don't either,« said Thomas, who was still standing just inside the door, following the meeting from a distance. »But I'm just wondering, what about the zoo?«

»Oh no!« squealed Kathrin. »Those poor animals! Who'll be looking after them?«

(to) sort out: in Ordnung bringen, klären, lösen

»Let's **sort** that **out** later,« said Ben. »First I'd like to hear what else has happened. Because I think there could be several more problems ahead.«

How right he was! No sooner was Ben himself about to start telling them about what had happened at the shopping centre, his search of the stockrooms, and the cold store that wasn't there, than Thomas shouted: »Hey, there's a blue light! An ambulance with its blue light flashing!«

All thirteen children joined Thomas at the door of the hall.

It couldn't be true. There weren't any grown-ups around, so no ambulances could be driving through town, let alone with blue lights flashing. Or did that mean the grown-ups were back?

There was nothing Ben wanted more just then.

The ambulance drove up and stopped. Right in front of the hall. Ben couldn't believe his eyes: Miriam was **at the wheel**!

at the wheel: am Lenkrad

She climbed out as if it was the most natural thing in the world for her to be driving an ambulance around town with its blue light turned on. All the children **gaped** at her, motionless. Thomas was the first to pull himself together.

»Since when could you drive?« he asked.

»I learned once at this really good **rave**. Tell you about it later,« Miriam answered him back. »Now we have to see about the sick people.«

»Sick people?« cried Frank. The side door of the ambulance opened and Jennifer climbed out.

»We went to the hospital,« she said. »Luckily there were only three kids there. Two of them have just had their tonsils out and one's had his appendix out. He's on the stretcher in the back there.« And Jennifer told them the whole story: how Miriam suddenly remembered her brother, how they'd both cycled to the nursery and found the whole place empty. She went on to her idea that they might find out more at the hospital, and described how she and Miriam had cycled there. But the hospital seemed empty, too. There was no one in the babies' ward or any of the other main wards either. Jennifer and Miriam had searched the whole place until finally, in the ear, nose and throat department, they found the two fourteen-year-olds whose tonsils had been removed, and then – another half hour later – they'd found George, whose appendix had been taken out a week earlier and who was in a single room on his own.

»So now tell me where the little kids are, Ben,« Jennifer finished.

(to) gape: den Mund aufsperren, angaffen

rave: die Party, die Fete

Ben thought hard.
»I just don't know,« he said at last. »It's like this: although the computer game is about children – they have to save the city – there are no really little kids in it at all. The grown-ups disappear, but there aren't any little kids to start with. That probably makes sense. I guess they've disappeared along with the grown-ups.«
»What are you going on about? What computer game?« asked Thomas, speaking for everyone. They'd all found out that the grown-ups had gone, but what that had to do with some computer game was a mystery to them.
»I get the feeling you four know more than we do,« Kathrin put in. »I think it's about time you told us.«
Ben, Frank, Miriam and Jennifer thought so, too. Now was the time to put the others in the picture. They all sat down by the open door of the ambulance, so that the sick boys could hear all about it, too, and Ben told the whole story from the beginning: about the computer game he'd swapped with Frank, about the error that had crept into the game, the disappearance of the grown-ups, the meeting in the school yard that morning – of course most of the others had been there, too, but not the hospitalized trio – the chaos in the shopping centre, the quarrel with Kolya, who was obviously planning to create more **havoc**, and finally the unsuccessful search for a cold store containing fresh food.

havoc: das Chaos, die Verwüstung, der Schaden

»And Jennifer just told you about looking for Miriam's

brother, and how it seems all the other little kids are gone as well,« Ben finished his long explanation.
All the children were silent. The situation was clear now: they were alone in the city and they didn't know how to keep it going. Food was running low because hundreds of excited children had been throwing it at each other. There didn't seem to be any huge supermarket with fresh food and a cold store. In the middle of all this chaos Kolya was on the loose somewhere, threatening to do even worse than he'd done already, and everyone was afraid of him. The animals were still around, including a whole zoo, and no one knew where food for the animals was going to come from. And now they had three sick kids on their hands. But worst of all was the uncertainty. How long was all this going to last? Would the grown-ups ever come back at all?
It was the smallest boy who put this all-important question into words. As the others told their stories he began crying miserably and put his head on Miriam's shoulder, sobbing.
»Aren't my parents ever coming back?« he **wailed**. »I want my mum and dad!«

(to) wail: jammern, klagen

Frank couldn't stand this. »The situation isn't hopeless, really,« he tried to comfort the child.
All the children looked at Frank in surprise. They had just been thinking exactly the opposite. Frank didn't let the baffled faces put him off.
»Listen,« he went on, »that's the way I often feel in a

match or something – now I've really blown it, I think, I've lost, not a chance now. And just when I'm thinking that, there's my trainer standing on the sidelines yelling, *Great, Frank, you're going to do it!* Karate, athletics, it's all the same. And then I remember what my strong points are, I tell myself I just won't give up, and I've often gone on to win.«

»Well, congratulations!« said Miriam sarcastically. »What a shame we don't have any hot-shot trainer around.«

»So what are *you* planning to do?« Frank snapped back. »**Twiddle your thumbs** and starve to death?«

(to) twiddle one's thumbs: Däumchen drehen

The moment he said that the little boy began howling again.

»Idiot!« Miriam hissed at Frank. »Maybe we ought to stop and think about getting the grown-ups back.«

Now it was Miriam who had everyone looking at her in surprise. »And just how, may I ask, are you going to do that?« asked Frank ironically.

Miriam went pale around the nostrils and **shrugged**. She didn't have an answer.

(to) shrug: die Schultern zucken

Ben came to her aid. »I can only tell you what happens in the computer game,« he began cautiously. »The kids in the game have to stick together, help each other, and survive in the city. That's how you reach the higher levels. And sometime you win the game and the city's back to normal. Or that's what the game description says anyway. I've never got that far yet.«

»You mean we have to go through all the adventures

in the game to bring the grown-ups back?« Jennifer asked.

»That's right,« Ben told her.

»And no one knows how to play it?«

»Correct.«

»Oh, wonderful!«

»That's just what I meant!« said Frank. »I meant we have to remember our strong points. For instance, no one knew you could drive, Miriam. And suddenly you come zooming up like Niki Lauda, bringing in the sick kids so they don't have to lie around alone in hospital. Who knows what the rest of us can do?«

Miriam was not sure who Niki Lauda was, but she felt flattered. Yes, Frank was right. She'd done well with the ambulance. Even big, strong, brave Frank the great sportsman couldn't have made such a good job of getting into the ambulance and driving off!

»Okay,« grinned Miriam **cheekily**. »What can you do, then?«

cheekily: frech

»I could see Kolya off, for instance, if he tries making more trouble,« Frank replied at once.

»I saw him about an hour ago, by the way,« said Thomas. »At the filling station. They'd nicked a couple of swish cars. They filled up and then they shot off. Squealing tyres and all that. Probably racing each other. I don't think I want to know the result. I bet they can't drive as well as Miriam.«

Miriam's **prestige** had risen visibly since she drove up in the ambulance.

prestige: das Ansehen, die Achtung

»We don't have to bother about them for the moment,« said Ben. »But it would be a good idea to split up and do different things. Kathrin, seeing you have your horses to look after anyway, maybe you could take on the zoo as well? Go and take a look first, see what the situation is like there and what we need to do about it.«

»Sure!« Kathrin beamed. Animals were her passion. She'd have gone to the zoo straight after the meeting to help the poor creatures there, even without being asked.

»Let me come, too,« asked the little boy. He didn't want to look silly again, the way he had with the TV sets. He thought it would be better to join one of the bigger children, and anyway he'd always liked going to the zoo.

»Great!« said Miriam. »That's what we'll do! We'll split up the jobs that have to be done, and then we'll win the stupid game and bring all this to an end!«

The others happily agreed. »Let's go, then!« said Kathrin. »Where do we meet again?«

The children all thought about it.

HQ: Abk. für **head-quarters** = das Hauptquartier, die Zentrale

»It would be best to have some kind of **HQ**,« suggested Jennifer. »A place where we could all go to find out what's going on.«

»Well, there's here at school,« said Miriam. »School is the place where we usually learn the news.«

»Good,« agreed Ben. »We can find everything we need in the school office, and Thomas has the key.«

»Yes, that can be our HQ!« said Thomas, pleased that his keys were coming in so useful. »And the caretaker's apartment is right beside it. It's empty now, so we can use it.«
»And put the sick kids there. They'll be close to us and quite comfortable, too,« said Jennifer.
»But we don't have a key to the caretaker's apartment, do we, Thomas?« asked Frank.
»That shouldn't be any problem,« said Thomas. »I have any number of other keys at home. One of them will probably fit. If not we can use a **skeleton key**. I have that at home, too, of course.« Thomas was getting prouder and prouder to think that his collection, so often **mocked** by the others, was really appreciated now. He immediately volunteered **to hold the fort** in the newly chosen headquarters.
»What else is there to do?« asked Miriam. If everything was working out pretty well, she wanted to be part of it, too.
»Well, you're the only one who can drive, Miriam,« said Jennifer. »The two of us could drive into town and collect any food those idiots have left after their food fights. Then we can build up a food stock of our own here in school. After all, Thomas has keys to all the rooms.«
At the mention of food Kathrin remembered the animals again. »I'm off to the zoo with this little boy. I know where to find you again now.« She took the child's hand and set off.

skeleton key: der Dietrich

(to) mock: verspotten
(to) hold the fort: die Stellung halten

»My name is Max,« protested the child, who didn't like being described as »this little boy«.
Thomas went to fetch his collection of keys so that he could open up the caretaker's apartment. Miriam, Jennifer and two other children left in the ambulance **to forage** for food.

(to) forage: herumstöbern, aufstöbern

»And what do we do, Ben?« asked Frank.
»Let's go and get my computer,« suggested Ben. »After all, the whole thing began with that computer game. Maybe we can bring it to an end without having to go through all the adventures.«
He had no idea just how, but he was determined to try everything that might possibly get the grown-ups back in town.

Fire!

Frank and Ben had gone a couple of streets in the direction of Ben's home when the two of them heard a loud crash.
»A **window pane** somewhere,« said Frank, and thought no more of it. It was nothing unusual at school to hear a window pane breaking. It happened at least once a week; no one bothered about it except for the caretaker, who regularly went scarlet in the face and lost his temper. Broken windows were an everyday event.

window pane: die Fensterscheibe

But this was different. There were only children left

in town. If something happened now, it was up to them to deal with it. There were no caretakers to do the job, no cleaning ladies to clear the broken glass away, no grown-ups at all to make sure nothing worse had happened.

If something went wrong anywhere it was all up to the children – it was their business.

Ben said nothing, but turned at once and ran in the direction of the sound. Frank, rather surprised, followed him.

Ben didn't need to go far to find the source of the crashing noise. The bar only a few hundred metres away had no window panes left at all. The noise was still going on inside: a crashing and smashing and clinking as if the toughest action film of the century was being shot inside the little bar. There were five Mercedes 300s parked outside its door. Several boys surrounded by a number of beer bottles were sitting on the car roofs and **bonnets**. They were shouting and laughing, drinking from their bottles from time to time, and then throwing them half-empty through the windows of the bar.

bonnet: die Motorhaube

No doubt about it: this was Kolya's gang having their idea of a good time.

Ben stayed on the other side of the street and stared at the spectacle. Frank joined him. He saw Kolya come out of the bar with a broken chair-back in one hand.

»That old fool won't half be surprised!« shouted

Kolya; he meant the bar owner. »He chucked me out of this place three times because he said I was under age. Now he'll see what I can do! He'll have a job clearing up this lot when he gets back!«

»*If* he gets back,« muttered Ben quietly to himself. Then he turned to Frank. »Maybe the owner will never come back – or any of the other grown-ups. Kolya doesn't seem to realize that.«

(to) be as thick as two short planks: dumm wie Bohnenstroh sein

»Kolya is **as thick as two short planks**,« said Frank. »Who knows what . . .«

But he got no further.

»Stop that, you idiot!« Ben suddenly shouted at Kolya as loud as he could. The big boy was just going back towards the bar with a burning rag in his hand.

He's never going to . . .: hier: Er wird doch nicht etwa . . .

Frank gasped. »**He's never going to** set the place on fire?« Without stopping to think twice, he raced across the street to the other side. Four boys immediately jumped off their stolen cars and grabbed him. Ben ran to his friend's aid, but he, too, was held captive. There were just too many of them. Ten boys held Ben and Frank and watched, laughing, as the first flames burst out of the bar. Kolya came running out, **cackling with glee**. Then he saw the two **captives**.

cackling with glee: teuflisch kichern
captive: der Gefangene

»Hey, look at that,« he grinned. »The part-time cops are here again.« Slowly, he sat down on the only white Mercedes – obviously the car he had kept for himself when the rest of the gang were dividing up the **loot**.

loot: die Beute

»Give the little goody-goodies something to remember us by!« he said. The other boys didn't need to be told twice. They began **laying into** Frank and Ben at once. The two friends hadn't the slightest chance against the superior numbers of Kolya's **thugs**. Their hands were tightly held, but they tried to kick out as best they could in self-defence, and warded off at least a few of the **blows**.

The whole thing lasted only two or three minutes – although it felt to Ben like several days – and then he and Frank were lying on the pavement, **gasping**, **groaning** and bleeding. Kolya told his thugs to be off. The boys all got into the limousines and drove away. Ben and Frank struggled slowly up. The bar was in flames in front of them.

»We must fetch help,« groaned Ben.

»Where from?« asked Frank, who had managed to get to his knees but was still clutching his stomach.

They hadn't thought of that. Everyone at the meeting had been so pleased to think they had fixed on a proper headquarters, but no one had thought of making a note of the caretaker's phone number, or the school's. And very likely Thomas wouldn't be back with the keys yet anyway.

Even if he was, what could Thomas do at their HQ? He wouldn't have known how to reach any of the others either. They simply weren't prepared for this kind of thing.

Indeed, they hadn't planned for emergencies at all.

(to) lay into sb: auf jdn losgehen

thug: der Schläger

blow: der Schlag, auch: die Handgreiflichkeit

(to) gasp: nach Luft schnappen

(to) groan: stöhnen

Suppose Miriam can't drive as well as we all thought and she has an accident? What's Kathrin found at the zoo? Does she need help as well? But all these questions going through Ben's head were no use at all at the moment.

»We have to get out of here!« **croaked** Ben. All his bones ached, especially in his left arm. *I hope it's not broken*, he thought.

(to) croak: krächzen
(to) ache: schmerzen

By now the fire was burning so fiercely that it was getting dangerously hot for Frank and Ben on the **pavement**. Frank carefully got to his feet and supported Ben when he saw that his friend was obviously worse injured than he was.

pavement: der Bürgersteig

They limped to the other side of the street. What on earth could they do? They couldn't just stand there and watch the fire spreading. There was no point running back to school. There'd be no one there but the three sick boys, and maybe Thomas if he was back. All the rest had gone off.

»There's two boys in our parallel class who are members of the volunteer junior fire-fighters,« said Frank suddenly. »I wonder where they are at this moment?«

Ben **saw the ghost of a chance**.

(to) see the ghost of a chance: eine Chance wittern

»If we don't know where they are, we must show them where *we* are!« he said in excitement. »There's two or three hundred kids on the loose in this town – if we can manage to get a fair number of them here maybe we'll have a chance of putting out the fire!«

»How are you planning to do that?« asked Frank. Just then a burning door-post crashed into the street.

»Some will come anyway,« Ben suspected. »Look at all this dark smoke. They'll be able to see it all over town! As for the others – well, we must find some way of attracting their attention.«

Ben and Frank looked down the street, hoping to spot something that might help them.

»I know!« cried Frank suddenly. »It may not work particularly well, but it'll be better than nothing.«

Before Ben could ask any questions Frank had run off. Although running wasn't really the word for it, Ben thought. Frank was hopping along the street with a peculiar sideways movement. *Like a crab on* ***springs***, thought Ben. And he was **poking** his head forward in a funny way, too. Suddenly he stopped, crouched down for a moment, took a mighty leap and landed on the bonnet of a parked car.

spring: die Sprungfeder
(to) poke: strecken

The car began hooting its horn, on and on and on.

Now Ben saw his friend's idea. Frank was hopping along the row of parked cars, looking for the little stickers on the windows warning that there was a security alarm.

As Ben realized what he was doing, Frank struck lucky for the second time. He jumped on another car and set its alarm off. Now there were two of them hooting. Frank rapidly hopped further; a third horn began to sound, then a fourth. It was only a few minutes before Frank had set the alarms of ten or eleven cars off. A ear-splitting concert of hoots was echoing down the street. It must be audible several blocks away. The noise and the smoke rising from the fire, which was getting blacker and blacker, must surely alert people to the fact that something was wrong here.

(to) pant: keuchen, schnaufen

Frank came back, **panting** for breath.

»Can't think of anything else at the moment!« he gasped. He **mopped** the blood off his face with his sleeve. He'd been so busy setting off alarms that he had quite forgotten how badly his nose and lip were still bleeding. Half his face was smeared red. Ben looked at his friend in horror, but Frank only smiled.

(to) mop: wischen

»Looks worse than it is,« he told Ben. »I've had this sort of thing happen often enough in karate.«

Ben did not find that particularly reassuring. He was alternately using his right hand to support his bruised left arm – *or was it broken?* – and mop the blood from his own nose. Both hurt horribly, not to mention the other bumps and bruises on his body. He felt his knees were swelling up. Ben would have liked to crawl into a bed somewhere and burst into tears. The **hooting** echoed around him. The bar was still burning brightly. It wouldn't be long before the flames reached the drugstore.

hooting: das Gehupe

The drugstore! That was an idea!

»We have to get to the drugstore!« shouted Ben.

»Are you crazy?« shouted Frank back in surprise. »It'll be burning, too, any minute!«

»That's why we must hurry! Come on!« And Ben was already limping towards the drugstore. Once he reached it, he picked up the broken chair back that Kolya had left lying in the street, put all his remaining strength into his sound right arm, and smashed the display window of the drugstore.

»What are you looking for in there?« shouted Frank, who had followed his friend.

»Rockets!« Ben shouted back.

»What?« Frank didn't get the idea at all.

»I always buy my New Year fireworks in here,« croaked Ben back. Shouting against all the hooting horns was making him **hoarse**. »I bet they didn't sell out and they'll be keeping the rest until next New Year. We can send the others a signal with rockets.«

hoarse: heiser

»Why didn't I think of that?« wondered Frank. »You stay here,« he told Ben. »The way you're **limping** you'll be much too slow. The fire's coming closer already. Go and find some bottles to stand the rockets in – there's plenty lying around the street – and I'll go in and find the fireworks!«

(to) limp: humpeln, hinken

Frank disappeared into the drugstore through the broken window. He rapidly went through the cupboards behind the counter. *No, they wouldn't be keeping the rockets here. There's probably a cellar*. Frank ran into the room behind the shop. His first glance fell on a board by the back door with keys hanging from it. *Good thing grown-ups are always so neat and tidy*, thought Frank. Because there were several keys, each with a neat **label** identifying it. Frank took the two keys labelled *Back Door* and *Cellar*. He heard

label: das Schild, die Aufschrift

something fall to the floor, crackling, in the bar next door. Hands trembling, Frank opened the back door, and with one stride he was out in the yard. Frank looked at three heavy steel doors. *One of them must lead to the drugstore cellar*. Unfortunately there were no labels here. Frank tried the first one. *Wrong, of course!* And the next, but the cellar key didn't fit that one either.

Out in the street Ben had set up fifteen bottles in a long row by now. He glanced nervously at the drugstore. **I hope Frank does it.** Ben was very worried about his friend. The flames from the bar were burning higher and higher. They were already blackening part of the outside wall of the drugstore.

I hope Frank does it: Ich hoffe, Frank schafft das.

»What's going on?« called several voices at this moment. Ben turned and saw five children running towards him. In a few words he explained the situation even before they had quite reached him. Ben added that there must be several other children in town who were members of the junior fire-fighters.

»Sure,« said one boy; Ben had an idea his name was Torben. They'd played football together once.

»The boy who lives next door to me is,« Torben said. »Norbert, that's his name. I saw him just now. I've an idea he was thinking of going to the fire station to try one of the big trucks. When the grown-ups were around the younger volunteers were never allowed to touch them.«

»Good!« said Ben, pleased. »How can we find him?

We need him here at once. With any other fire-fighting friends of his, too.«

»Sure, we'll fetch him!« said Torben. »Who'll come with me?«

Another boy and a girl immediately **volunteered**, and the three of them ran straight off.

(to) volunteer: etw freiwillig tun, sich melden, bereit erklären etw. zu tun

One boy and one girl stayed with Ben. »What can we do?« they asked.

»Right now we can only wait until Frank comes out of the drugstore,« said Ben. »Or we could stand up a few more bottles.«

Frank had finally found the cellar, on the other side of the third door.

A whole series of **crates**, bags and cartons stood around in the **cramped** space. The few shelves were **crammed** full, but most of the stuff was all over the floor. *So much for grown-ups being neat and tidy*, thought Frank. *When no one can see them they're as bad as they say we are*. He made his way past the cartons, **glancing at** open ones here and there and reading the stickers on crates and packets: he found eau de toilette, deodorants, soap, toothpaste, fly-spray, perfume, hair colours, bath foam, even liquorice sticks. But no fireworks. Frank stopped . . . *They'll be keeping the rest until next New Year*, that was what Ben had said. *Meaning for a whole year. If they won't be wanted for a year then they're bound to be in the furthest corner*. Frank thought hard. Whereabouts in this cellar would he himself put some-

crate: die Kiste
cramped: hier: eng

crammed: voll gestopft

(to) glance at sb/sth: einen kurzen Blick werfen auf

thing he didn't need for another year? *Right up on that shelf*, Frank decided.

The cellar might be quite small, but its ceiling was high. Too high for Frank, anyway. He couldn't see what was on the top shelf. Quickly, he grabbed two of the stoutest-looking crates, piled one on top of the other and stood on them. Now he could see the things on the top shelf – but they didn't contain fireworks either.

On to the next set of shelves – no, to the last one. Frank decided to try right at the back, the top shelf in the furthest corner. **Dragging** the two crates after him, he **stacked** them **up** again, jumped on them, took a look and . . .

»Got them!« Frank let out a shout of **delight**. He saw two cartons which clearly contained fireworks, and the coloured stickers left no doubt about it. Well, he could *see* the cartons, yes, but he couldn't get his hands on them. In front of this particular shelf stood towering **piles** of crates, cartons and bags. Frank had neither the time nor the inclination to clear the whole lot away and then stack his two crates neatly up again. Instead, he jumped up on the untidy piles, slipped a little way back on a smooth bag of something, but **clutched** the shelf quickly with one hand, and then **clambered** the remaining few metres to the top of the mountain of cartons and bags. Once there, Frank cautiously stood upright, holding the shelf with his left hand and reaching for the first carton of

(to) drag: ziehen

(to) stack up: stapeln

delight: die Freude

pile: der Stapel

(to) clutch: schnappen nach

(to) clamber: kraxeln, klettern

fireworks with his right hand. Just a little further, and then he could get a proper grip on the carton at last. Frank hauled the carton down from the shelf. It was lighter than he'd expected, which meant he tugged so hard that the carton hit him in the face. Frank jumped back, his right foot slipped, his left foot went the other way and he automatically bent backwards. In one last attempt to save himself Frank let go of the shelf, his left arm **flailing** through the air. But it was no use. Frank lost his balance, fell head first into the mountain of cartons, pulled down a second shelf with his feet, it crashed on top of him, and finally he landed head first in a carton full of toilet paper.

Well, that was a fairly soft landing anyway, thought Frank. Then he felt something slippery and cold running down his back. Feeling behind him, he found that his fingers were covered with the slippery stuff. He raised his head with difficulty from the carton of toilet paper, pushed some boxes aside with his slippery hand, scrambled down from the mountain of cartons and got to his feet. He realized there was a peculiar smell around: sweetish, no, a bit **astringent**, kind of fresh and yet with a touch of **mustiness** about it. All those things together. *Perfume*, thought the horrified Frank, and now he saw, just where he had been lying, a carton **seeping** moisture from goodness knew how many broken perfume bottles in front of him. Right next to it a **gooey** white substance was **oozing out** of a broken tub labelled »**Soft Soap**«.

(to) flail: fuchteln

astringent: herb

mustiness: der Modergeruch

(to) seep: sickern

gooey: dickflüssig, klebrig

(to) ooze out: hervorquellen

soft soap: Schmierseife

»Oh *yuk!*« said Frank, realizing that this disgusting, gooey mixture of slippery soft soap and perfume had got all over him while he was head down in the carton of toilet paper.

All the same, one carton of fireworks lay at his feet. The other was still on the shelf. Frank felt not the slightest wish to get that one down, too. He quickly checked the contents of the carton in front of him. *What luck, it's the one with rockets. Fifty of them at least!* Frank, delighted, put the carton under his arm and decided it was time to get out of there. *If he could still get out of there! Who knew how far the fire had spread by now?*

Up in the main drugstore again, Frank realized he hadn't a moment to lose: half the place was on fire already, and here he was with a carton of fifty rockets under his arm!

Frank took a deep breath, or as deep as he could in the **soot**, smoke and heat, **thrust** his head slightly forward – like a bull about to attack – and sprinted through the drugstore. With a **bold** leap through the broken display window, Frank's adventure ended. There he was out in the street again. He'd made it!

Frank saw that Ben had been busy, too. Ten children were standing on the other side of the street, shouting and waving enthusiastically at Frank **in relief**. And beside them stood a large, bright red fire engine! Frank, astonished, ran to join the others.

»Yuk! You smell like all my aunties put together at Christmas!« Ben greeted him.

soot: der Ruß
(to) thrust: stoßen, strecken

bold: kühn, verwegen

in relief: erleichtert

»Very funny,« said Frank **sourly**. He didn't care for the smell of his involuntary perfume shower himself, but there was nothing he could do about it at the moment. »Tell me what's been going on here, why don't you?«

sourly: griesgrämig

Quickly Ben told him how the five kids had come around the corner, how one of them knew Norbert of the volunteer junior fire-fighters and had gone straight off to find him.

Sure enough, Norbert and three of his friends were at the fire station. They'd been planning to get to know their way around the big fire engine for once – but they'd never dreamed they would be called out so quickly to their first real emergency.

The four excited boys had **scrambled** into their fire-fighting clothes and gone off with the fire engine to join Ben. Six months ago, luckily, one of the four, Martin, had **persuaded** his team leader to let him try driving a fire engine on the volunteer fire-fighters' practice field; it was one of the old, much smaller engines that had been taken out of service. The drive here had been much more difficult and also bumpier than that, but somehow he had managed it – now, when it really mattered.

(to) scramble: klettern, kraxeln, hasten

(to) persuade: überreden, überzeugen

»Terrific!« said Frank. »Looks like I didn't need to fetch the rockets at all!«

»Yes, you did,« said Norbert. »We four know what to do about this fire, we've connected up the hoses to the fire hydrant already, but there's a lot more to be done. We need to get as many people as possible here to lend a hand.«

»Here goes, then,« said Frank, and he began handing out the rockets.

Ben and the others had stood over forty bottles up by now. They put a rocket in each bottle while a girl called Marina ran across the street to the drugstore. She took off the scarf she was wearing round her neck and cautiously held it in the flames. When one end of the scarf caught fire she came back with it. »I guessed none you had a light!« she said, looking around.

She took her burning scarf down to the end of the row of bottles and started lighting the rockets. One after another they **whooshed** towards the sky. Now the children were standing in a group, as they might at any firework display, heads back, accompanying the brightly coloured explosion of every rocket with a loud »Ooh!« and »Aaah!«

(to) whoosh: zischen, rauschen

For a moment everything else was forgotten.

»Look at that blue one! I had one of those last New Year's Eve!« cried Marina, pointing up in the air.

»Wait a minute, the really expensive one is coming next,« said Rolf, who had said nothing so far. »My Dad gets one of those every year. It looks terrific. Little sparkling silver stars and then a big green flash.«

»I like the big round red ones best,« said a girl called Silvia. »They light up our whole part of town.«

»Those aren't rockets. They're fired from **flare pistols**,« said Norbert the junior fire-fighting volunteer, who knew all about it and was happy to set the others right.

Silvia was not impressed. »What a pity,« was all she said, shrugging.

The sight would have made any grown-up's heart stop with horror: there, in what had once been a homely little shopping street, the remains of a bar were **smouldering** in the **twilight**. Next door a drugstore was burning, while ten enthusiastic children were standing beside an out-of-action fire engine, gazing at the fireworks they had set off themselves. Here and there cars were parked, black with soot, still accompanying the show with loud hooting of their horns.

But the plan worked.

Children came running up from all directions. Twenty, thirty – no, more like fifty kids arrived within a few minutes, Ben guessed.

»What's going on?«

»Who fixed this firework show?«

»Why didn't anyone tell us?«

»Has it only just started?«

All the children were shouting **in confusion**.

»There's a fire!« Ben and the others kept telling them. Only then did most of the children see what was going on in the street. At first they had all just put their heads back to watch the rockets go up, never notic-

flare pistol: die Leuchtpistole

(to) smoulder: schwelen
twilight: die Dämmerung

in confusion: durcheinander

ing that a store was burning, and the bar was already entirely burnt out.
Norbert and his three friends stood in the middle of the street, giving brief instructions to all the new arrivals.
The children were much too excited to ask any more questions. They let him divide them into teams, ran to their posts and listened to the instructions they were given. Most of them were told: Hold the hose.
»Now!« shouted Norbert, one hand raised in the air. He brought it down. Martin turned on the water at the hydrant. Immediately the limp, flat hose-pipe swelled to a thick, fat, round, gigantic snake trying to **coil** in all directions at once. About fifty children clung to the rebellious monster as it tried to get its own way.

(to) coil: sich winden, kringeln

»Hang on to it!« shouted Norbert. »Don't let go!«
Peter and Mark, two more of the junior fire-fighters, clung as hard as they could to the head of the **twitching** snake, from which a rushing jet of water was now **cascading** in a wide **arc** and falling on the burning drugstore.

(to) twitch: zucken
(to) cascade: herabregnen
arc: der Bogen

The battle with the flames lasted two hours, and by then the children had won. The bar was completely wrecked, and they hadn't been able to save the drugstore either, but no other buildings had been damaged. The walls of the local fishmonger's shop were black with soot, but the shop itself was alright. The fire was out!

Exhausted, all the children sank to the ground just where they stood. No one said anything; the operation had taken too much out of them. They were wet through with water from the hose, they were dirty and worn out, but they felt proud and happy. They'd done it – all by themselves, too, without needing help from a single grown-up.
»You know what?« Frank suddenly asked. »I suggest we all go to the swimming pool now and then back to our HQ.«
The swimming pool – that was a great idea!
All fifty yelled with enthusiasm, and exhausted though they were, they jumped up and ran **cheerfully** off. On the way to the pool, Ben and Frank told the others about the HQ set up in the school.
The two friends looked at each other with satisfaction. Today had been an all-round success. Not only had they put out the fire started by Kolya, the action in which they'd all co-operated had seen their group grow from a mere fourteen children to over sixty. If they all worked together, they could control the problems of the city. Ben and Frank were sure they could. *In the computer game you'd earn 17,000 points at one go for an operation like this*, Ben thought.
But it was a long, long time since **Kid City** had been only a computer game – all of twenty-four hours ago.

cheerfully: gut gelaunt

Time to Relax

Within ten minutes the children had reached the municipal swimming baths. They were lucky that the grown-ups had disappeared at a time of day when the baths were still open. That meant the doors were unlocked, and the electric light and everything else they needed was on.

The children raced into the baths, ran past the changing rooms and made straight for the showers. Every time they usually came here to swim they groaned about being made to shower first, under strict supervision. But today was different. After their fire-fighting operation it was a huge relief to get under the warm shower and scrub off the dirt and soot. They didn't even stop to undress first. Frank in particular was glad of the chance to get rid of that slimy soft soap and the revolting smell of several mixed perfumes. Of course they had a good water-fight under the hot showers. You turned the shower to very cold, **scooped** up a handful of water and splashed it over the back of the person in the next shower when he wasn't expecting it. It was great to hear the yells of your victims echo through the **tiled** room! Fifty children **screeching** and squealing, shouting and screaming in the showers.

(to) scoop: abschöpfen

tiled: gekachelt
(to) screech: schreien, kreischen

A pity the swimming-pool attendant wasn't around. He'd have been horrified – though of course no one really missed him.

After about ten minutes no one could stick it out under the shower any more. It was lovely to see the swimming pool they'd been longing for lying there like a silk carpet, just waiting for fifty **riotous** schoolkids to turn its peaceful water into a **choppy** sea. Funny that none of the other children in town had thought of coming here for a swim, thought Ben, but it was a fact: they were the first.

Frank immediately made for the ten-metre diving board. Ben was happy with the three-metre board. *Mustn't overdo it,* thought Ben. A dive from a height of three metres would be enough for him. All three boards – three-metre, five-metre and ten-metre – were **cordoned off** with red and white striped tape as usual, but no one minded that today, since Mr Timm wasn't around.

Mr Timm, a big, strong man, at least 1.90 metres tall and broad-shouldered, was the swimming-pool attendant. All the children in town knew him and none of them liked him. They called him Terrorist Timm.

»Have you showered?« was always his first question the moment you put your nose out of the changing room. Once you'd cleared that **hurdle** by showing him your wet hair and you were on your way to the edge of the pool, he barked out a second **indistinct command**. It meant, »Don't do that!«, and what you mustn't do was **dive** into the water from the edge of the pool. Diving was allowed only from the diving boards. But if you so much as **ventured** even to look

riotous: wild, übermütig
choppy: aufgewühlt

(to) cordon off: absperren, abriegeln

hurdle: die Hürde

indistinct: undeutlich, genuschelt
command: der Befehl
(to) dive: springen, tauchen

(to) venture: unternehmen

at those tempting boards from a distance you had Terrorist Timm snarling a loud but indistinct »Closed!«, meaning that the diving boards were off limits for the moment. And it always seemed to be the moment.

»You know, I almost miss Terrorist Timm!« Frank called from the ten-metre board down to Ben on the three-metre board. Frank would have loved to see Mr Timm's face as he watched fifty children breaking all his rules just as they pleased.

»Watch out, dive-bomb coming!« yelled Frank from the ten-metre board. He was about to break the most sacrosanct rule of all and dive in backwards, knees drawn up and both hands clasped round them. It was really impressive: when you hit the water a huge fountain shot up above the side of the pool, and a big wave washed over everyone standing there. The fact that the only person standing there was usually Mr Timm made this dive special fun. That was why it was strictly forbidden, and if you dared to do it you were usually banned from the pool for two weeks as a punishment.

Not that that made any difference. Terrorist Timm banned children from the pool for a week at every opportunity, with the result that he could never remember which kid wasn't allowed to swim at any given moment. So all the children always went in whenever they wanted.

Frank did his backwards dive, the wave washed over

the side of the pool, and five more boys copied him. The floor beside the pool was several centimetres deep in water now, making it difficult to see where the pool itself left off. If only Mr Timm could see this! Fifty children **squealed** with **enthusiasm**. They had all jumped into the water fully dressed, which was strictly forbidden, too. You weren't supposed to go swimming except in a proper costume or trunks, and a bathing cap. Of course none of the children had their bathing things with them after their fire-fighting operation, and they didn't like to swim with nothing on; the boys didn't want to strip off in front of the girls, and vice versa. So they all jumped in just as they were – and anyway their clothes had been washed in the showers with them. Everything and everyone had got dirty fighting the fire. Ben had never understood why grown-ups were always so keen on washing things separately.

(to) squeal: kreischen
enthusiasm: die Begeisterung

He looked at his watch. It showed that it was 15.10 hours in New York, 4.10 hours in Tokyo, 23.10 hours in Moscow, and 21.10 hours here in the swimming pool.
»Oh no!« groaned Ben. »Back to headquarters! The others will be waiting,« he called to Frank.
»You're right,« Frank agreed, climbing out of the water. »After all, we were really only going to fetch your computer.«
»Come on, back to HQ, then,« said Ben.
»Everyone back to HQ!« shouted Frank, loud enough for everyone to hear him.

»But we can't go back to school like this,« objected Norbert, splashing his way like a penguin over to Ben and Frank in wet socks, wet jeans and wet woolly sweater.

»You could at least have taken your socks off,« replied Frank, the only one who had swum barefoot and bare-chested. His clothes had been too sticky from all that soft soap for him to keep them on. No one else had thought of keeping at least some of their clothes dry, they'd just jumped into the water as they were.

All the other children had climbed out of the pool now. Water was flowing, trickling and dripping off them as if everyone of them was a walking waterfall.

»Listen, there's a department store just round the corner,« Martin remembered. »I bet we'll find dry things to fit us in there.«

slug: die (Nackt-) schnecke

Like a huge slimy **slug** leaving a wet trail behind it, the crowd of fifty children set off for the store.

Ben found some blue jeans, a brightly coloured T-shirt and a black sweater with a colourful graffiti pattern on it. Frank sprinted off to the sports department and snapped up the new self-ventilating jogging suit that was so expensive he'd never dared ask his parents for it. The other children found something to wear, too, after a brief search. They all knew there was something they'd always wanted, and now they had only to reach out and pick up the clothes of

their dreams without the **hovering** presence of their parents – who would have groaned in horror at the sight of the prices. All fifty kids were dressed from head to foot in new clothes within half an hour. However, none of them wanted to abandon their old things, so they found plastic bags at the main cash desk and put their wet clothes in those.
»Right,« said Ben. »Now let's get back to HQ.«

Jennifer was standing at the school gates, looking anxious.
»Good heavens,« she groaned as she saw the fifty children coming. »Where did all the others spring from? What happened? We've been waiting for you for hours!«
»Take it easy.« Ben tried **to soothe** Jennifer. »We'll tell you all about it inside.«
»Let's go to the **small hall.** We're cooking a meal in there,« Jennifer told him. Sure enough, there was a delicious smell of noodles and tomato sauce in the small hall where people could play and eat their sandwiches during break.
»Very timely,« said the delighted Frank. »**I'm as hungry as a hunter.**« But he had to wait a little longer. The other children in the small hall rushed up to Ben and Frank, **deluging** them with questions.
The two friends told the whole story of Kolya and the bar, how Kolya's gang had beaten them up, then the fire, Frank's heroic operation getting hold of the fire-

(to) hover: hier: über etw. schweben

(to) soothe: beruhigen, beschwichtigen

small hall: Pausenhalle

(to) be as hungry as a hunter: einen Bärenhunger haben

(to) deluge: überschwemmen, bestürmen

works, the great fire-fighting episode and all the fun they'd had in the swimming pool afterwards.
»Oh, honestly!« cried Thomas **indignantly.** »Here we are slaving away to build up stocks of food and cook supper, while you lot are having fun in the swimming pool!«
»Do be quiet,« Miriam snapped. »After what they've been through I'd have gone swimming first thing too. A pity I wasn't there. But you could at least have phoned.«
That was a useful reminder. Ben pointed out to the others that although they'd set up their headquarters here, which was a good idea, no one had thought of taking a note of the phone number and fixing up a warning system to get help fast in an emergency. He told them how he and Frank had been left bleeding in the street, and the lack of any system for calling for help could almost have been **fatal** to them.

fatal: verhängnisvoll, tödlich

»I've an idea,« said Norbert, when Ben had finished what he had to say. »We have walkie-talkie radios in the fire-fighting service. We could put one in the headquarters here, and separate groups going around town could take the others with them. Though I think we may not have quite enough – ten or so at most. And I guess some of them aren't in working order.«
»But they'd be better than nothing,« Jennifer said.
»The hospital!« exclaimed one of the boys Jennifer

and Miriam had brought in the ambulance. Thomas and some of the other children had brought mats from the gym into the small hall and made a bed for the three invalids, so that they wouldn't have to lie around alone in the caretaker's apartment at mealtimes. It was George, the boy whose appendix had been taken out a week ago, who spoke up now. »The doctors in the hospital always have **beepers** on them. They carry them in the pockets of their white coats. And if someone urgently needs the doctor the beeper goes off and the doctors know they're wanted. My doctor's beeper usually went just when I'd asked him a question – and then he had to rush away. For instance, I wanted to know how the beepers actually work, but the doctor didn't even have time to tell me. And I'd have been really interested to know, because everything else was dead boring in that hospital. I *still* don't know, I'm afraid.«

beeper: der Piepser

»I do, though,« said Thomas. »I even found one of those things lying about once. It was broken, and I didn't know what it was, but I just brought it home. Because the great thing with something that looks broken is . . .«

». . .that it's for free and you only have to pick it up,« chanted Ben, Frank, Jennifer, and Miriam in chorus, not to mention fifteen other children who knew Thomas and his maxims.

»Could you please keep to the subject?« Jennifer asked him impatiently.

snide: abfällig

crossly: böse, verärgert, gereizt

telephone switchboard: die Telefonzentrale

I'm ravenous: Ich habe einen Bärenhunger/Riesenhunger

Thomas hesitated for a moment, but then went on. Never mind their **snide** remarks! Who'd found all the keys to school and made it possible for them to have a headquarters here? His collection had come in really useful!

»Well, so I took it home with me and asked my Dad what it was. And he explained it to me. That's all I was going to say,« replied Thomas, shouting against the angry chorus.

Jennifer impatiently drummed her fingers on the back of a chair. »Well?« she asked **crossly**. »Aren't you going to tell us how those beepers work? Wasn't that what you were about to say?« She shook her head, baffled. *Sometimes Thomas's ideas are scattered as far and wide as all the stuff he's so keen to collect,* she thought.

Feeling that she had trapped him, Thomas went red. »Yes, okay,« he stammered. »Right, well, there has to be a central control unit – something like a **telephone switchboard** – and it puts out signals and the beepers receive them. That's really all there is to it. But I've no idea how big the control unit is. Maybe it's just a small box and we can bring the whole system here from the hospital.«

»Can't we discuss all that later?« said Frank. »I really am **ravenous**!«

»There's only one little problem. We didn't know you'd be coming back with so many people,« Miriam pointed out. »We'll have to cook a whole lot more now.«

»Anyone know how many noodles we need to put on?« asked a boy standing by the stove.
»And how to make enough tomato sauce?« added a girl standing beside him.
»To be honest I don't think we have enough anyway,« said Thomas. »I made a note of it: forty packets of noodles, that's what we have here.«
»What, only forty packets?« asked Martin, who, as a member of the fire-fighting volunteers, had often helped to serve goulash at shooting matches. So he had some notion how much food large parties of people could eat. »Why only forty?«
»Why only forty?« snapped Miriam. »Because we thought forty packets of noodles was plenty, that's why. We did the journey three times anyway with all the other stuff we fetched. Who was **to lug** all of it here?«

(to) lug: schleppen

»Okay, okay.« Frank tried to pacify her. »That'll probably do for today. But tomorrow we absolutely have to get more **supplies**. There's nearly eighty of us now.«

supplies: die Vorräte, der Nachschub

»Yes, Frank's right. *We* can do it tomorrow,« Martin offered. »We'll take one of the fire engines and pack it full of stuff.«
»How much more now, then?« This question came from the stove again.
»Oh, **chuck** it all in. We can eat it!« Frank called back.

(to) chuck: schmeißen

The children at the stove took the biggest pans they could find in the school kitchen cupboard, filled them halfway up with water and added the remaining thirty-four packets of noodles to the six already cooking. They did the same with the tomato sauce. They'd already heated up ten cans of sauce; now they opened another fifty. There were four huge pans on the big stove in the hall where volunteer parents usually cooked for children who stayed at school for lunch: two pans of noodles and two of tomato sauce. All four were **full to the brim**. After just five minutes the first two pans began boiling over. Bubbling and hissing, hot water splashed out of the pans of noodles, flowed over the stove and ran down the cupboards to the floor, foaming. A boy and a girl were leaping about among the sixty empty tomato sauce cans.

full to the brim: randvoll

»Help!« shouted the boy, Matthias. »The noodles are after us! Ouch, that water's hot!«

»And listen to the tomato sauce **gurgling**!« squealed the girl, whose name was Marion. A big splash of tomato sauce shot out of the pan and **sailed** over the other pans straight onto her sweater. Matthias and Marion leaped back, shrieking, **left** the bubbling, gurgling pans **to their fate** and got out of the way.

(to) gurgle: blubbern, gluckern

(to) sail: segeln

(to) leave sth to its fate: etw dem Schicksal überlassen

»For heaven's sake turn the stove off. It's heating up all the time!« yelled Martin, **charging** bravely at the knobs of the stove as if he were fighting a fire. But it wasn't so easy to put the tomato sauce out of action. It fired its next shot straight at Martin's left eye. Martin **yelped**, put his hands in front of his face, trod on one of the cans, slipped and crashed against the

(to) charge: angreifen

(to) yelp: aufjaulen, aufschreien

stove with his **behind**, upsetting a pan of noodles with a loud **clatter**. Luckily the pan fell sideways on the counter top and not straight on Martin. Just as well, but several hot splashes of cooking water from the noodles reached him all the same. He yelled, but still he managed to turn the knobs of the stove to zero. A real fire-fighter takes the job seriously. He was just about to shout a relieved »Done it!« to the others when a shower of icy water hit him. Martin screeched, spat, gasped, and held his arms over his head to protect it.

»Max!« he heard the other children call behind him. Max was just a metre away from Martin. While all the others had been following Martin's battle against the tomato sauce with bated breath, none of them noticed what Max was up to. He had grabbed one of the buckets of water standing around – afterwards, no one could really remember what they were there for – and thrown the contents over Martin.

»I only wanted to help,« little Max defended himself. »Cold water's good for burns, my mother says so.«

»Thanks, Max,« said Martin appreciatively, »but if you carry on like this I'll more likely be drowned than burnt.«

All the children fell about laughing. Martin struggled slowly up, and Norbert **perched** Max on his shoulders. »Max, I hereby appoint you **deputy fire chief**!« shouted Norbert. »You can put out fires for people who hold swimming certificates!«

behind: der Hintern
clatter: das Geklapper, das Geschepper

(to) perch: setzen auf
deputy fire chief: stellvertretender Feuerwehrhauptmann

(to) simmer on a low heat: auf kleiner Flamme kochen

muddle: das Durcheinander

on the counter top: auf der Theke, hier: Küchenschrank

(to) scrape: kratzen, zusammenkratzen

gymnasium: die Turnhalle

»I think we ought to be a bit more methodical with this cooking,« said Jennifer, as everyone laughed. »The pans ought to be only half full and **simmering on a low heat**. That means we'd better cook and eat in two shifts. First everyone whose surnames begin with the letter A to K eats, then everyone from L to Z. But now let's clear this mess away so we can move around the stove.«

»Yes, Madam Chairwoman!« said Frank. »Okay, even though my surname is Zöllner so I'll be one of the last to eat. But I guess I don't have any choice in this chaos.«

»How right you are,« smiled Jennifer, who could always solve any **muddle** with a few energetic suggestions, even if they did sound rather like orders. They all set about putting her plan into practice.

»What do we do about the noodles **on the counter top** and the floor?« asked Miriam.

»Put them back in the pan!« Jennifer decided. »Well, that's what they always do in restaurants, it's just that no one sees it.«

Miriam giggled, **scraped** the noodles off the floor and put them back in the pan.

Water!

Ben was the first awake. He looked around the big **gymnasium**. About eighty children were still sleeping soundly nearby. No one had felt like going home to sleep there alone yesterday evening. It was much nicer to spend the night together in the gym. Somehow they all felt safer there, and most important of all, no new information would escape them that way. The school, as Miriam kept saying, really was the place where all news came in. So after supper the children had put mats down on the floor of the gym, they ran home for their sleeping bags, and then they all lay down in the big hall. It was well after midnight before they were all finally asleep. They **nestled** together in groups, talking over the day's events.

Ben looked at his watch. It was only seven in the morning. All the same, he couldn't sleep any longer, although he was sure he hadn't **dropped off** until four. There was just too much to be done. There was to be a meeting at ten, and they'd decide who should do what. What were the next things to do? First they'd have to hear a few more reports: from Kathrin about the zoo, from the people who'd gone looking for food and so on. They hadn't felt like **tackling** all that the evening before. They'd just enjoyed a good meal together, then spent some time fetching their things and making themselves as comfortable as possible in the gym. No one felt like sleeping with the horrible neon lighting on there, but they didn't want complete darkness either, so they had brought clip-on lights and extension cables. Some had brought their portable CD players and were listening to their favourite music. A couple of the children

(to) nestle: kuscheln

(to) drop off: hier: einschlafen

(to) tackle: in Angriff nehmen, bewältigen, hier: sich Gedanken machen über

even danced until two in the morning. Thomas and Miriam had gone to the food store and found peanuts and salty cocktail sticks for everyone.

Ben looked out of the window at the school yard. Sixty pullovers and pairs of trousers dangled from washing lines stretching right across the yard. Their wet clothes from the swimming pool should be dry again soon.

»Hey, Ben, are you awake?« whispered Jennifer, a couple of beds away. She scrambled over to Ben, sleeping bag and all.

»What do you think is going to happen today, Ben?« she asked. »I mean, how does the game itself go on?«

»I don't know,« Ben told her. »I think we can look after ourselves okay for a while – finding food and drink and so on. But I don't know what's going to happen in the long run. We'll probably reach the last level of the computer game. I think that's our only chance. But I don't know what the rules are at that point myself. To be honest, that sometimes scares me.«

»It's a funny thing«, said Jennifer, »I've sometimes felt cross with my parents even though they're really very nice. But I didn't want any more to do with them than strictly necessary, I wanted to be left alone. And now I *am* on my own, and it feels kind of weird.«

»It certainly does!« agreed Ben. »It's only now we really notice what grown-ups do for us. I mean, it's amazing the way the whole city functions. Electricity and water and food supplies and all that. And look at us – we can create chaos just cooking noodles.«

Jennifer nodded thoughtfully. »Yes, always being responsible for things can really **get a person down**. You should have seen me and Miriam yesterday having to think of everything we need to eat. Goodness, there's so much to bear in mind! It was really awful.«

(to) get sb down: jdn fertig machen

»I believe you. I wouldn't have wanted that job either. To be honest, the sooner I'm back with my mother the better. Even if I do always have to be home for supper at six. Right now I wouldn't mind that one bit if I didn't have to think of everything for myself,« Ben **admitted**.

(to) admit: zugeben, eingestehen

»We have a few years to go before we're grown up ourselves,« Jennifer **pointed out**.

(to) point out: feststellen, klarstellen

They both fell silent. Here and there in the gym someone stretched in a sleeping bag, a head came out from under a blanket, there was a brief, whispered »Morning« in the big hall, groups of two or three children still nestled in their sleeping bags talking quietly.

»Listen, Ben,« Jennifer began again, »I wanted to say I think you and Frank were really great yesterday, dealing with the fire and Kolya, and getting all the kids here and so on.«

»You were great, too,« replied Ben, rather awkwardly. »I mean, the way you got the chaos under control yesterday evening, when we were cooking supper, that was terrific.« Ben glanced briefly at

Jennifer out of the corner of his eye and then looked down at his knees again.

Jennifer smiled. »I kind of like you, Ben,« she whispered in his ear.

Ben went red and smiled, too. »And I like you,« he stammered. At this moment he couldn't think of anything else to say – but he didn't need to.

»Interesting things you miss in the morning if you sleep too long,« remarked Miriam suddenly. Jennifer and Ben turned in alarm.

turtledove: das Turteltäubchen

»Good morning, you two **turtledoves**,« chuckled Miriam.

»Don't be so silly, Miriam,« said Jennifer at once. »You're imagining things.«

»Oh yes, of course,« grinned Miriam. »But you know what an interest I take in people's relationships. Has this one been going on long?«

(to) be out of one's depth: überfordert sein

»Has this *what* been going on long?« asked Ben, **feeling out of his depth**. He was glad that Frank was stretching and waking up beside him now.

awkwardness: die Betretenheit, die Verlegenheit

»Anything wrong?« asked his friend. The air was suddenly full of **awkwardness**.

»No, everything's okay, Frank,« said Ben. »Why don't we find some breakfast? How about that? I'm getting hungry.«

»Sure!« said Frank, looking at Miriam and Jennifer, who had been in charge of finding food supplies. »What is there to eat?«

»Delicious things,« Miriam told him. »Cornflakes,

nougat cream, muesli, jam and lots of chocolate bars.«
»Chocolate bars?« asked Frank, puzzled.
»Yes, chocolate bars, of course!« beamed Miriam. »I always eat chocolate bars for breakfast, don't you?«
Frank made a face. »What, no scrambled eggs?« he asked.
»Scrambled eggs?« It was Miriam's turn to be baffled.
»That's right,« said Frank, »scrambled eggs. I could really do with some. Didn't you bring any eggs?«
»No.« Miriam examined Frank as if he were an extraterrestrial. How could anyone eat scrambled eggs first thing in the morning?
»Luckily!« said Jennifer. »Do *you* fancy cooking about eighty helpings of scrambled eggs? Cooking supper yesterday evening was enough for me.«
»I suppose you're right again.« Frank gave in. He'd just have to manage without scrambled eggs in the morning for a while. It was a tough life without parents around.
An hour later they were all sitting in the small hall happily munching cornflakes with **UHT milk**, muesli and bread with jam and nougat cream. Miriam and Jennifer had forgotten to bring any butter or margarine, but no one particularly minded. They just spread a rather thicker layer of nougat cream, which was an excellent **substitute**. After all, there was no one around to tell them not to eat so much of it.

UHT milk: die H-Milch

substitute: der Ersatz

»Hey, Kathrin, what's it like at the zoo?« Thomas suddenly asked across the table. Unintentionally, he'd opened the meeting.

»It's still okay, just about,« said Kathrin, »but we'll have to keep an eye on things. The two tigers are sort of **pacing up and down**. They must be as hungry as hunters.«

(to) pace up and down: hin- und hergehen

»How can tigers be like hunters?« asked Max, sitting next to Kathrin.

»Oh, Max, it's nothing to do with real hunters, it's just a saying,« explained Kathrin, although now she thought about it the expression struck her, too, as a little silly. But she went straight on. »I've made a list of all the animals in the zoo. Now we'd better think how to feed them. But like I said, we must do something for the tigers pretty quick. They badly need something to eat.«

»Cat food,« said Max.

»What?« asked Kathrin.

»Cats need stuff out of cans, or that's what they're always saying on TV,« explained Max. »And tigers are kind of big cats, right?«

»You're getting me down, you and your TV,« exploded Kathrin. »You were like that all the time in the zoo – ooh, look, Baloo the bear, and there's Flipper the dolphin, and look, Simba the lion, and goodness knows what else. Don't you have anything at all in your head but TV, you stupid boy?«

Hurt, Max bit into his roll and strawberry jam.

Miriam thought this was too much. Whenever the little boy said something they all turned on him. Anyway, Miriam didn't see what Kathrin had against television. Miriam herself didn't watch animal films and cartoons like Max, but if she put together all the music video-clips she saw **in the course** of a week it would add up to several hours. To be honest, the TV in her room was always switched on when she was in.

in the course: im Verlauf

»Okay,« Miriam said to Kathrin, »so what do *you* suggest we feed those tigers?«

Max looked up.

»Fresh meat, of course!« said Kathrin firmly. »What a stupid question! Tigers need fresh meat.«

»Right,« said Miriam, standing up. »Let's go.«

Max looked from Miriam to Kathrin and back.

»Go?« Kathrin was surprised. »Go where?«

»Go and fetch your horses!« snapped Miriam.

Kathrin still didn't understand.

Miriam took a couple of steps towards the exit. Then she stopped and turned casually. Max stopped chewing.

»We'll just slaughter one or two of your horses, right?« said Miriam, looking perfectly serious. »Well, they're the only fresh meat we have available right now!«

Kathrin leapt to her feet, screeching, »Are you crazy? My horses . . . for those stupid tigers to . . .?« Kathrin couldn't even bring herself to say it.

slyly: gerissen, verschmitzt

(to) wink: zuzwinkern

(to) make up the quarrel: versöhnlich sein

crockery: das Geschirr

»Cat food after all, then?« said Miriam **slyly**.

»Yes, of course,« Kathrin was quick to agree. »A thousand times sooner than my horses!«

»Right.« Miriam sat down again, and **winked** at Max. He beamed all over his face and took another good bite of his roll and strawberry jam.

»I suggest we divide up the jobs for today,« said Ben, finally beginning the meeting officially without interrupting breakfast. Frank helped himself to another large plate full of cornflakes. Miriam took her fifth chocolate bar.

»First,« began Ben, »who'll see to the animals in the zoo?«

»What is there to do there?« someone asked.

Kathrin spoke up again. »Well, the food isn't so urgent, although we really ought to give the tigers something to keep them happy. But they all need water to drink. I'll go back to the zoo. Coming, Max?« She looked at Max, ready **to make up the quarrel**.

»Right,« said Max, and ten other children volunteered, too.

»We'd better get those walkie-talkie radios before anyone starts out,« Norbert suggested. »We don't want anyone hurt, like Ben and Frank yesterday.« He and Martin stood up at once and left the meeting, saying they'd be back soon.

»Maybe we ought to clear up a bit here at HQ,« said Thomas. He pointed to all the **crockery** standing around. Everywhere you looked there were yester-

day's plates, glasses, spoons, forks, and the four huge saucepans with noodles and tomato sauce dried on them, all pushed into great piles to make room for the breakfast things.
»Though I don't know who's going to wash all these dishes,« added Thomas unhappily. He'd never seen so much dirty crockery all at once.
»If you ask me, the idiots who were throwing food about in the shopping centre ought to do the first shift,« said Jennifer.
The children who had been there looked awkward. By now they understood the devastating consequences of their battle in the shopping centre. It had been so tempting – and so many of the others had joined in. All the same, no one dared object to this idea.
»At least there's a dishwasher here,« said a boy called Christopher.
»Where?« asked Thomas, who hadn't yet found any such thing.
»No idea,« admitted Christopher. »But my mother's one of the parents who help out in the school canteen, and she said they have one. I'll look for it and organize the dishwashing. Who else is volunteering?«
Rather reluctantly, eight or nine children spoke up. Another five said that when Norbert was back with the radios they'd go and look for more **provisions** with him. Ben and Frank were finally going to get

provisions: der Vorrat (hier: an Lebensmitteln)

Ben's computer. What with the fire, they hadn't got around to it before. Miriam and Jennifer said they would go out with the ambulance to find cat food for the tigers. One by one all the children offered to do various jobs.

Norbert and Martin came back with the walkie-talkie radios and handed them out to the separate groups, who went happily off. Thomas went to hold the fort in the school office. He'd volunteered to receive information from the separate groups and pass it on to the others if necessary.

Christopher had found the dishwasher, and was starting **to rinse** plates under the tap. »That's what you do, you rinse the worst of it off first and then stack it in the machine,« explained the dishwashing expert. But it didn't work the way Christopher had expected. No water came out of the tap. Christopher turned the tap off and then on again: still no water. *I don't believe it*, he thought. Hands on his hips, he looked at the dry tap in despair. He thought for a moment, but nothing occurred to him except to turn the tap on yet again. It was as **obstinate** as ever and still didn't give out any water. Meanwhile Torben was **scrabbling** about on the floor in search of the **stopcock**. After a while he found it and tried it. »Can't be that,« he said. »The stopcock's not turned off.«

Thomas made a note of it in a large book he'd found in the school office. He had torn out the used pages and started the book again by writing **INCIDENTS** OF

(to) rinse: abspülen

obstinate: widerspenstig

(to) scrabble: krabbeln

stopcock: der Haupthahn, der Absperrhahn

incident: das Vorkommnis

SPECIAL IMPORTANCE on the cover in fat red felt pen.

»Group Four calling HQ,« the radio in front of Thomas on the desk suddenly **squawked**. Thomas put his felt pen down and pressed the Send button on the radio. »HQ here. Come in Group Four.«

Group Four consisted of six children who had gone to find some toys, because of Astrid's suggestion at the meeting that smaller children aged six to nine should have a playroom in one of the classrooms. That way the little kids would be all together, the bigger children wouldn't have to keep looking out for them and, best of all, the little kids wouldn't be in the way when there was something important to be done. At first the smaller kids protested indignantly. They wanted to be around when there *was* something important to be done. Max in particular pointed out at the meeting that he had been very helpful the day before counting the animals in the zoo for Kathrin's list. He had to count the **chimps** eight times, for instance, to find out just how many there really were, because they kept chasing around their **enclosure** so fast that he never knew which chimpanzees he had counted already and which he hadn't. Kathrin did agree that Max had tried hard, but added that it had been a great nuisance for her, having to find out where he was all the time. Once he tried talking to a parrot when he was supposed to be counting mountain goats; another time, while Kathrin thought he was inspecting the zebras

(to) squawk: quäken, kreischen

chimp/chimpanzee: der Schimpanse

enclosure: das Gehege

with bated breath: mit angehaltenem Atem

on the other side of the zoo, he was watching **with bated breath** to see how long a bird-spider could sit on a rock without moving.

After Kathrin had said her piece, the majority were in favour of the idea of a little kids' playroom, and the older children promised that it would be full of brand new toys from the department stores. After that the little kids couldn't resist the temptation, and agreed to the playroom. But at the same time they were given the right to join in what the bigger children were doing for at least three hours a day – of course they imagined that this would be exciting things like putting out fires, while the bigger children had in mind jobs like dishwashing or tidying up.

»Group Four here,« said Astrid again over the walkie-talkie, after Thomas had replied. »On the way to the shopping centre we divided up for a while to go and feed our pets at home. We're all back together now – and everyone says there's no water in the taps at home.«

»That's funny,« said Thomas. »Same thing here at HQ. No water, or at least not in the small hall.«

»So what are we going to do?« asked Astrid.

Thomas looked in his big book to see what Group Four had set out to do in the first place. *Collect toys*, he read, and went back to the radio. »Well, do your job first, collect those toys.« He thought for a moment. »Can you still hear me, Group Four?« he asked.

»Yes, we're still on the line,« Astrid replied.

»Maybe,« said Thomas, »it wouldn't be a bad idea to test all the taps you see. Can you try a few other **connections to the mains** as you go around?«
»Yes, of course,« said Astrid. »We'll look in all the shops, see if they're connected and whether the water's running. Over and out.«
»Right. I'll tell the other groups to do the same. Then report back in. Over and out,« Thomas cut the radio connection.
Then he pressed another button the way Norbert had shown him. Now he should be connected up to all the groups at once. »HQ here, HQ here. Calling all groups, calling all groups,« Thomas began.
The groups reported in.
»This is a general announcement. There's no water here in school or in several other buildings. Please try all connections to the mains you pass. I repeat, please try all connections to the mains!«
»We already said we would!« said Astrid.
»I know,« said Thomas.
»Then why radio us and tell us to test the mains all over again?« asked Astrid.
»Because it was a general announcement to everyone,« replied Thomas, crossly.
»Yes, but we knew already,« Astrid insisted.
»I know you knew,« said Thomas, patiently trying to explain. »But if I press the button to call everyone, then I call you, too.«
»Isn't that a bit **daft**?« inquired Astrid.

connections to the mains: hier: die Wasseranschlüsse

daft: blöd, albern

Thomas was at a loss, until he remembered what grown-ups always said in such circumstances. »It's a matter of technology,« he cheerfully told Astrid. Even she would have to accept that.
»Stupid old technology!« replied Astrid over the walkie-talkie. »Okay, we'll try all the taps. Over and out.«
»That's what I said,« replied Thomas.

(to) retort: erwidern, zurückgeben

»We know you said it,« **retorted** Astrid.
Thomas groaned out loud. »Over and out!« he groaned, and quickly pressed the Off button. For a while the radio couldn't pick up any more messages.
But half an hour later they were coming in to HQ thick and fast. Group One, which was Kathrin's group at the zoo, reported in, sounding agitated, »Hey, Thomas, there's no water anywhere here at the zoo. We were going to give the animals water, but there's none in the pipes. All the taps are dry. Even the fresh water supply in the aquarium has failed. This is a disaster!«
Group Two, Miriam and Jennifer, had much the same to report. »We passed the fountain in the market-place, and that's not playing any more. We'll take the cat food to the zoo now. Then at least we can feed the tigers and hope the water problem will soon be cleared up. And we'll try to get food for the birds and so on from the zoo shop. We'll have to see what we can find there.«
Thomas passed the information on to Group One at the zoo. Kathrin and the other children were glad

they'd be able to help at least some of the animals a bit. But the most interesting report came in from Group Three: Norbert and the children who'd gone with him to find food.
»Hi, Thomas! We just stopped at a hydrant and tried it to see if it was working. Even the hydrant had no water. You know what that means?«
Thomas didn't know.
Norbert explained. »If there's no water from a hydrant then there's none anywhere at all in the district. The water supply has dried up all over town. This isn't a failure in some of the mains, it has to mean that the whole city's water supply has been shut off at the waterworks!«
Now Thomas realized just what that meant: if there was no water in the mains anywhere in the whole city, they were in serious danger! No one can survive without water.
Thomas got up from his desk and **paced up and down** the school office, very upset. What was he to do? Should he pass on the information to all groups and maybe set off a panic? On the other hand, he couldn't solve the problem alone. If it could be solved at all, they'd all have to think about it together. Thomas radioed a message to Ben. *Group Five – fetching computer.*
»Group Five here. Ben speaking,« Ben called in.
Thomas told him what the other groups had reported in from the city, and passed on Norbert's theory.

(to) pace up and down: hin- und hergehen

»Just a moment.« said Ben. He turned the walkie-talkie off and told Frank. Frank looked at Ben without a word.

»You're thinking the same as me, right?« Ben asked. Frank nodded.

»This could be tricky,« muttered Ben to himself. Turning his radio to Send again, he called in. »Thomas, pass this on to all groups: we'll hold an important special meeting. In the main hall in an hour's time. Never mind what the groups are doing, they'll have to drop it and come to the hall. Frank and I will be there, too, maybe with interesting new information. Over and out.«

Thomas didn't know what might be behind that, but **he didn't stop to wonder**. Instead he did as he was told, and informed all the groups. *Let's hope*, thought Thomas, *let's hope Ben and Frank really do have a good idea. Because without water we'**re done for***.

not to stop to wonder: nicht weiter darüber nachdenken

(to) be done for: erledigt sein, am Ende sein

Kolya Again

There was a lot of excited talk and noise in the main school hall. Norbert had told the others that he **suspected** there was no water in the whole city any more. Kathrin was going on at the top of her voice about the animals in the zoo, and Thomas was **gloomily** prophesying that in his view they'd all be done for if the water problem wasn't solved very soon.

(to) suspect: vermuten

gloomily: niedergeschlagen, bedrückt

»I'd rather drink juice anyway,« said Max. »And I don't think washing is all that important.«
»Oh, for goodness' sake, Max,« replied Thomas. »We still need water. Think of the fire Kolya started. Imagine if we hadn't had any water. Something like that could happen again any time. And what are you going to cook with – **orange squash**? Those noodles we had yesterday, for instance – we boiled them in water. It's the same with rice and potatoes. You can't cook them in Coca-Cola. We even need water for mixing the instant mashed potato. We have some UHT milk, but it won't last forever. And then there's the dishwashing.«

orange squash: der Orangensaft

»All the same, Max has a point,« Miriam put in. »If we go to all the shops selling things to drink we can get by on bottled mineral water for a while. Only for a while, though.«
»And the animals will have died of thirst by then,« wailed Kathrin. »You can't just put a bottle of mineral water each in front of the tigers and zebras and mountain goats and so on. They drink far more than that. The mineral water will never be enough. And there's the fish and the sea-lions, too. We can't fill up their pools with sparkling water!«
»Like I said, we have a real problem,« Thomas repeated.
»Too right we have!« said Ben behind him. He and Frank had just come into the hall.
»There you are at last! Where've you been?« cried Jennifer. »Do you have any news?«

»Yes, but it's not good,« Frank began. »We're late because we've been to the waterworks. And guess what we saw there?«

Never mind the suspense!: Mach es nicht so spannend!

»**Never mind the suspense**, get on with it!« Miriam snapped at him.

»Several cars parked right outside,« said Frank.

»So what?« said someone. »There are cars parked everywhere. Even standing in the middle of the street.«

»Let me finish,« said Frank. »One of the cars was a white Mercedes. Remember what we told you about the fire?«

»Kolya!« said Jennifer.

main lever: der Haupthebel
water supply: die Wasserversorgung

»Right!« Ben agreed. »Kolya is occupying the waterworks with his gang. He's found the **main lever** for the city's whole **water supply** and turned it off.«

»He must be out of his mind!« said Norbert furiously.

»Did you see Kolya?« asked Jennifer.

(to) be on watch: Wache halten

(to) be armed to the teeth: bis zu den Zähnen bewaffnet sein

»Well, of course we went into the waterworks. Or rather we tried to,« said Frank. »But they were **on watch** at the gate. All the gang are carrying baseball bats, and some of them even have gas pistols. Crazy. They'**re armed to the teeth**.«

»What for?« asked Norbert.

»It's simple,« said Ben. »Kolya wants to rule this city. He came to the gate and told us this was his big chance, no adults around any more. He was going to be real ruler of this city, and if we didn't agree and recognize him as our boss we could die of thirst for all he cared. That's what he said.«

There were indignant protests in the hall. »Never!«

»Has he been watching too many westerns or what?«

»I always thought he **was a few sandwiches short of the full picnic**.«

»If I could just get my hands on him . . .«

They were all yelling.

»Calm down,« shouted Jennifer. »**Bellowing** like this won't get us anywhere. Let's just stop and think what we're going to do.«

»Jennifer is right,« agreed Ben. »Well, we can't overthrow Kolya and his gang. They're very well armed – it's too dangerous. I'd say Kolya is capable of anything with a weapon in his hand.«

The others nodded. Yes, Kolya really might do anything at all.

»How many in his gang?« asked Thomas.

»We don't know. When he set that bar on fire there were ten or just over, but we saw at least twenty at the waterworks. And we don't know how many more were inside,« said Ben.

»I should think Kolya's gang has grown to forty or fifty by now,« said Frank.

»How many more kids are there in the city anyway?« Norbert wondered out loud.

Ben remembered standing on the shed roof, trying to make a speech to all the pupils. »There must have been two hundred in the school yard at the start of all this,« he estimated.

(to) be a few sandwiches short of the full picnic: nicht ganz bei Trost sein

(to) bellow: brüllen, grölen

»There were that many in the shopping centre too, I'm sure,« said Miriam. »If not more.«

Jennifer spoke up again. »There's about eighty of us. How many are we exactly? I guess it's about time we counted. Let's say Kolya has a gang of fifty. That means about half the kids are still running aimlessly around town. What are they actually doing?«

Many of the children shrugged their shoulders. »I saw some when we were out just now,« said Norbert. »Several on bikes, others probably **foraging** for something to eat in the restaurants and shops.«

(to) forage: herumstöbern

»Yes, and there were still a few **roaming around** the shopping centre when we went for the cat food.«

(to) roam around: herumstreunen

»I think we ought to tell all the kids we have our HQ here and recruit as many of them as possible before they join Kolya, too.«

There was general agreement to this idea.

»And don't forget we have the fire engines and the ambulance,« said Martin »They've got loudspeakers on board. We can drive around with them and make announcements to all the kids through the loudspeakers.«

The children applauded. That was a great idea! Miriam and Martin would do the driving. Norbert and Christopher said they'd broadcast messages through the loudspeakers.

»Okay, but that still doesn't solve the Kolya problem.« Jennifer had their attention again. »Even with a

hundred and fifty of us, Frank's right: we can't storm the waterworks. Kolya's gang is too big.«
»Then we'll have to do it **by cunning**,« said Ben.
The others fell silent. Easier said than done! They all thought hard. They knew that Kolya was **crafty**. Occupying the waterworks was a mean, **underhand** thing to do, but it did give him power over them.
»So how are you going to trick them all by cunning?« asked Frank.
»Those stupid idiots,« Miriam said furiously to herself. She was cross because *she* couldn't think of any solution, and at least letting off steam helped a little.
»If you ask me,« Ben said slowly, still trying to work it out, »it isn't so important how many there are in Kolya's gang, it's who they are.«
»What do you mean, who they are?« Frank couldn't make anything of that.
Miriam didn't quite see what Ben had in mind yet either, but she thought about the people she knew in Kolya's gang. »I bet you Siggi's with them,« she said at last.
»Siggi?« asked Jennifer. »The Siggi you went out with three times?«
»I did not go out with him!« Miriam said defensively.
»Oh yes, you did. Everyone knows you did,« claimed Jennifer.
»But not for long ,« objected Miriam.
Jennifer wasn't letting go. »You went out with him at least three weeks running!« she said.

by cunning: mit List

crafty: schlau, gerissen
underhand: hinterhältig

Ben rolled his eyes. »Does it matter who you went out with and how long?« he asked Miriam **irritably**.

irritably: gereizt

»I suggest we think who exactly belongs to Kolya's gang,« Miriam snapped back, »and that useless Siggi is sure to be in it. I promise you he is. He may be almost fifteen but he's about as bright as a child of nine.«

»Very funny,« said Max **grumpily**.

grumpily: mürrisch

»Sorry,« Miriam said quickly. »I didn't mean it that way. You're ten times cleverer than Siggi, honest.«

»So that's why Miriam went out with him three weeks running,« said Jennifer, chuckling until a sharp blow fell on her left arm.

»Stop that, will you?« **spat** Miriam. »He could be quite nice – at least, I thought so.«

(to) spit: hier: fauchen

»Oh, for goodness' sake,« groaned Ben. »Could you two please drop this? Miriam, tell us, how old is this Siggi?«

Miriam looked **blankly** at him. »Siggi is fourteen and he'll be fifteen the day after tomorrow, if you really want to know.«

blankly: verständnislos

Ben's eyes opened wide. He jumped off the chair where he had been sitting all this time, ran to Miriam, grabbed her by both shoulders and shook her. »He will? Are you quite, quite sure?« he shouted at Miriam. He was really worked up.

Flinching in alarm, Miriam pushed Ben away. »Of course I'm quite, quite sure. Well, it's like this, Siggi has always been kind of keen on me,« she admitted.

(to) flinch in alarm: erschrocken zusammenzucken

»That's why he asked me to his birthday party. The day after tomorrow in the **den** at his family's place. I said no, of course. But the way things look at the moment there won't be any party anyway.«

den: der Partykeller

»That's it!« cried the delighted Ben. »That's it!«

»That's what?« Frank and Jennifer looked at each other, baffled. What on earth had come over Ben so suddenly? The other children were getting impatient, too.

»Oh, come on, Frank!« Ben said impulsively. »Don't you remember what we saw outside that bar?«

»Oh yes,« said Frank. »We all know that. Kolya set the place alight.«

The others nodded. This was ancient history.

»No, no – before that!« cried Ben. »I mean what led up to it. Listen, it was like this: first Kolya wrecked the furnishings in the bar. Then he came out and said ›He'll get a surprise when he comes back.‹ He meant the owner of the place. And I said to you, well, if he ever comes back so will all the other grown-ups. That's how it was, right, Frank? Isn't that how it was?«

»Well, er . . . yes,« said Frank, not sure what Ben was getting at. »So what?«

Some of the kids sitting around grinned, but other were still staring at Ben, a question in their eyes.

»That's it!« said Ben happily »Kolya still hasn't the faintest idea what's really going on in this city! All he knows is that the adults have suddenly gone. **Leaving no trace**!«

(to) leave no trace: keine Spuren hinterlassen

»So do we know any more now?« asked Norbert.
»You bet we do,« Ben told him. »Look, I told you it's all to do with my computer game. Just how we don't know, but we can assume that's the general principle. Anyway, it all fits together: the grown-ups have gone, the most important things in this city are still working, the toddlers and babies have gone too, the animals are still around. It's just like in the **Kid City** computer game!«
»Even if it is,« objected Jennifer, slightly annoyed that everything was coming around to the subject of computers again, »even if it is, what good is that to us?«
Ben stood up, raised his forefinger and explained, as **portentously** as a head of state making a speech: »We know the rules! Kolya doesn't know them, because he has no idea this is all to do with the game!«

portentously: bedeutungsvoll, gewichtig

He sat down again to enjoy the others' reaction to his idea. It was disappointing. Eighty children just stood around looking at him inquiringly.
»So what do the rules say?« asked Jennifer, breaking this baffled silence.
Ben jumped up on his chair, **bowed** like an actor at the end of a play, slapped his forehead with the palm of his hand and cried, »Well, think about it, can't you? One of the rules tells us there are no adults left in the city.«

(to) bow: verbeugen

He paused for a moment to make sure his words really took effect this time, and then repeated, »No adults left in the city. No one of fifteen and over!

Don't you see what that means? Siggi will disappear at midnight tomorrow, on his fifteenth birthday. And Kolya doesn't know that, but we do!«

Miriam was trying to follow Ben's complicated train of thought. She wasn't doing too well.

»So *that* means what?« she asked cautiously. She looked around and saw how glad the others were that she'd asked this question.

»That means,« Ben began again, trying to be as patient as possible, »that means we'll make Siggi disappear. Or at least we'll tell Kolya so. We'll **trick** Kolya by going to see him and telling him to leave the waterworks. If he won't, we'll threaten to make his gang disappear – one by one. Kolya will say we're crazy and laugh at us. And then the first of his gang *will* disappear, at midnight. It'll be Siggi! And Kolya will think we did it.«

(to) trick: austricksen

An ear-splitting yell of jubilation rose in the hall. What a brilliant plan! That was the way to beat Kolya! None of the eighty children doubted it. »Well done, Ben!« »Hooray!« »Kolya, we're on our way!« they all shouted.

Norbert asked Thomas for the key to the storeroom, took a couple of boys with him and brought cola, fizzy drinks and peanuts into the hall. Christopher raced off to fetch a CD player from the gym. Now the celebrations could begin! Victory celebrations in a battle that was far from won yet – but no one was thinking of that at this minute.

Bluffing

aimlessly: ziellos

Next morning the children set about telling anyone still wandering **aimlessly** around town about the arrangements they'd made.

Miriam and Norbert took the ambulance and drove around the southern part of the city, while Martin and Christopher were going to cover the northern part with the fire engine.

As soon as Miriam had gone round the corner Norbert began shouting enthusiastically through the microphone. *»Hi, everyone! Come up to the school, that's our meeting point, okay? Everyone come along!«*

»Oh, great!« said Miriam sarcastically. »What a terrific announcement! What do you think they're going to make of that? You have to tell them why they're all to come, and what we're doing in school, and about Kolya and all that.«

»You do it yourself, then, if you're so good at it,« said Norbert, sounding offended.

touchy: empfindlich

»**Touchy**, aren't we?« muttered Miriam, taking the microphone.

»Your attention, please!« she began. *»Everyone listen! It's very important for all of you to come to the school. We have our meeting point there. And we have to think how we can get the water back again, because of Kolya. So come up to school as quick as you can. And bring sleeping bags with you!«*

Norbert was falling about laughing. »Oh, what a

great announcement!« he gasped. »You think anyone could make head or tail of that?«
Miriam put her tongue out at Norbert. »It was better than your garbage anyway,« she snapped.
»I don't think either of us did too well. Stop the car and let's plan the announcement properly. We could write it out first,« suggested Norbert, trying to make his peace with her.
Miriam stepped on the brake, changed down, went into neutral gear and put the handbrake on. Then she turned the **ignition key** to Off and let the engine die. She parked in the middle of the street. It didn't matter, since no other vehicles were driving around anyway, except for Martin in the fire engine, of course, and Kolya's gang if they were out and about with their stolen cars. But anyway there was a whole row of cars in the middle of the street.

ignition key: der Zündschlüssel

»Right,« began Miriam. »What do we say, then?«
She picked the ballpoint stuck in the ventilation panel on the dashboard and the notepad lying in the glove compartment with the walkie-talkie.
»I'd begin with *This is to everyone*,« said Norbert. Miriam wrote it down. »No, wait,« he corrected himself. »It'd be better to say *Everyone listen!* And then we'll say . . .«
». . . and then we'd better say who we actually are,« said Miriam. »How are they going to believe what we say if they don't know who's talking to them?«
That seemed like sense to Norbert, but he wondered

just how they should describe themselves. After all, they couldn't go through the names of all eighty children in their announcement.

»How about *Kids' Committee*?« suggested Norbert, after some thought.

(to) make a face: eine Grimasse schneiden
stuffy: gezwungen, steif

Miriam **made a face.** »*Kids' Committee*? We're not in your fire-fighting outfit here! It sounds so **stuffy**!« she complained. »Anyway, no one's decided to be a committee. It's a bit like Kolya wanting to be ruler and boss us about. Let's just say our own names. *This is Miriam and Norbert speaking*.«

Norbert was surprised to find it could be that easy. Miriam wrote it down.

»And then we'll say,« said Norbert, thinking some more, »then we'll say we're eighty children in all, and the others should come and join us.«

Miriam wrote that down. Then she stopped. »Don't you think we ought to say what it's all about first?«

Norbert agreed – and then the two of them sat for over an hour in the car, thinking about the announcement and discussing the text they'd broadcast through the loudspeaker system. Finally it was all written out. Miriam handed it to Norbert, who looked at their joint effort once again:

~~This is to everyone.~~ Everyone listen!
~~This is.~~ This is Miriam and Norbert speaking!
~~We're eighty kids in all.~~ We've joined up with a whole lot of other kids.

~~You should join us too.~~ We're inviting you to join us. Our meeting place is the school. ~~You can eat there, too.~~ We're all cooking and sleeping there, too.
And that's where all the news from the city comes in. ~~For instance.~~
The latest news is there's no water in town. ~~because.~~
The reason is that Kolya's occupied the waterworks. ~~Everyone come and~~
Now we have to think how we're going to get the water back on.
Everyone come up to school!

Norbert looked doubtfully at the piece of paper. »Who's going to be able to read that aloud, with all those crossings-out?« he asked.

»Oh, don't keep **picking holes**,« said Miriam. »It's about time we got going with this announcement.«

(to) pick holes: etw bemäkeln

Norbert sighed, and began hesitantly reading their carefully written text through the loudspeaker microphone. Miriam cautiously drove the ambulance past the cars standing in the street while Norbert kept repeating the announcement. After the tenth time he knew the whole thing almost by heart.

»This is working really well, Norbert,« said Miriam happily. »Look ahead there – there's several kids coming round the corner.« Sure enough, a group of five children was standing by the side of the street, eyes wide with surprise, listening to the announcement. The sight of them made Norbert spontaneously change the wording:

»Hi, everyone!
Yes, I mean you ahead of us there.
We need you, too!
This is Norbert and Miriam speaking.«

Then he went back to his original text. He could recite it smoothly now. At first the five children couldn't make much of the rest of the information from the loudspeaker. Of course they knew who Kolya was. Everyone at school knew that **creep**! But what was all this about water? Just who was meeting at the school? Never mind. If there were other kids there, at least they'd find out some news! The five children looked briefly at each other and ran off towards the school. Norbert and Miriam smiled, pleased.

creep: fieser Typ

»Yes, it's working,« said Miriam happily, and concentrated on not running into any of the other cars as she did a slalom course around the parked vehicles. Meanwhile Ben, Frank and Jennifer had arrived at the waterworks. They looked thoughtfully at the big, red brick building. Somewhere inside was the vital lever that supplied the city with water. And Kolya and his gang were guarding it. The big steel gate at the entrance was closed with a bicycle **padlock**, and just behind it, in the **porter**'s little lodge, sat Siggi on a wooden chair, his legs up on the brown desk. Jennifer

padlock: das Vorhängeschloss
porter: der Pförtner

spotted him at once. Siggi in turn saw who was at the gate. He jumped up, reached for the phone, dialled a short number, made a couple of excited remarks, rang off, sat down on the chair again and grinned at Ben, Jennifer and Frank outside. Less than five minutes later the three of them saw a **deputation** of six boys marching across the waterworks **forecourt** to the gate. Each of them had a baseball bat over his shoulder. Frank realized that two of them were also holding gas pistols. Kolya stalked across the forecourt surrounded by his armed **escort**.

»The great Kolya and his bodyguard,« whispered Jennifer. Kolya stopped about twenty metres behind the gate. His escort came to a halt, too.

»Nice day, isn't it?« Kolya greeted the three in an exaggeratedly friendly tone. »Had a good breakfast, or didn't you have any water?«

»Don't let that bother you, Kolya. We had an excellent breakfast. We certainly feel strong enough not to need any bodyguard,« replied Frank, looking **scornfully** at the armed boys. He added, nastily, »I'd no idea you were so scared I might hit you. Oh, well, poor little mummy's boy has lost his mummy now!«

Furiously, Kolya made for the gate. »One more stupid remark like that and you'll be for it! Remember what we did to you two outside that bar?«

Ben **flinched**. He was far from keen on a repeat of the experience.

But Frank replied, perfectly calmly, »Outside that

deputation: die Abordnung
forecourt: der Vorhof

escort: die Eskorte, der Begleitschutz

scornfully: verächtlich

(to) flinch: zurückzucken

bar? Oh, you mean when Ben and I were fighting ten of your gang and you ran away?«

looking menacing: bedrohlich aussehend

Looking menacing, Kolya came a step closer to the gate. »I don't mind opening this up if you dare come in. But don't ask me how you're going to get out again!« he snarled.

Jennifer tugged Frank's sleeve. They were here to trick Kolya by cunning, not get into a punch-up with his bodyguard. *Boys are so stupid*, thought Jennifer. *They always have to prove their strength. How can Frank be silly enough to provoke Kolya just now? He'll mess up our whole plan!*

She pushed in front of Frank. »We'd really rather know just what you want,« she said quickly, before Frank could challenge Kolya yet again.

»What I want?« Kolya laughed. »I made it clear what I want, or didn't your two heroes here tell you? I want what's due to me. I'm boss of this town. Everyone's under my command. And until you admit it there'll be no water. It's that simple.«

delusions of grandeur: der Größenwahn

»Simple?« asked Jennifer. »**Delusions of grandeur**, that's what I'd call it. What are you going to *do* when you're boss of this town?«

(to) be taken aback: erstaunt sein

Kolya **was taken aback**. He hadn't thought about that yet. He just wanted to be boss. What for was something he didn't yet know for sure. He didn't go in for difficult discussions like this, especially not with girls. He was obviously trying not to let the fact that he didn't have any plans to show.

»Well, there's always someone who's boss in any city,« he said, rather uncertainly. »And now the grown-ups have gone, so one of us has to be boss. And that's going to be me, before one of you nerds grabs the job. So what is there to talk about? It's perfectly simple.«

»Very simple,« said Jennifer, grinning. She had realized Kolya didn't have the faintest idea just why he was making these **demands**. »Not that I expected a clever idea from you.«

Kolya overlooked Jennifer's **snide** remark, and repeated his demands. »You can take your time deciding whether to accept me as boss. I suppose you know how long you can manage without water.«

»Longer than you think,« Ben said, joining in now. »After all, we're not living in the Sahara desert here. There's mineral water by the crateful in this town. We can get by on that for a long time. All the same, we'd like to have the mains water running again, if only for the animals in the zoo. They need water to drink.«

Kolya **nudged** one of his bodyguards with his elbow. »The animals in the zoo!« he said scornfully. All the boys behind the gate laughed. »What do we care if they die of thirst? But if you're so keen to save them, well, you only need to agree that I'm boss. So make up your minds.«

How can anyone be so heartless? Ben wondered. *As if the poor animals could do anything about our quarrels!*

Kolya was about to turn and disappear inside the red

demand: die Forderung

snide: abfällig, bissig

(to) nudge: stupsen, anstoßen

brick waterworks building again, but Ben called to him. »We made up our minds long ago!«

Kolya stopped and came a step closer to the gate again. »So you've decided to accept me as boss?« he asked hopefully.

»No way!« said Ben. »We've decided we're going to get the water back again – and you're the one who'll turn it on!«

(to) goggle: staunen, starren, glotzen

Startled, Kolya **goggled** through the gate. It took him some seconds to take in what Ben had just said to him. Then he got control of himself again. »And just how, if I may ask, do you think you'll do that?«

»Of course you may ask,« said Ben. »Easy: the situation's not exactly the way you think it is. *We* have ways of controlling *you*.«

In confusion, Kolya looked around, glanced at each of his bodyguard, and turned back to Ben. »*You* have ways of controlling *me*?«

»That's right,« agreed Ben, trying to sound as casual as possible. »We know now why the grown-ups disappeared. You don't. And the best part of it is, we know how to make it happen ourselves. We can make certain people disappear at certain times.«

Kolya looked Ben up and down suspiciously. He must be bluffing! »How could you ever do that?« he stammered, unable to think up any better question just now.

»That's our secret!« said Jennifer, pleased to see that the plan seemed to be working.

»If you know so much, how come you don't bring the grown-ups back?« asked one of the bodyguard.
Jennifer **cast a** desperate **glance at** Ben. She wasn't prepared for that question. What were they going to say now? Was this the end of their plan?
But Ben answered quite calmly. »Yes, we know how to make people disappear. We can do it that way round ourselves. But we haven't found out how to do it in reverse yet. We can't bring anyone back because we don't know so far where they've actually gone.«
That sounded convincing – if only because it was the truth. Ben's whole story was true except for the little bit about being able to make people disappear. That was bluff – but of course Kolya didn't know it.
Uncertainly, he asked: »But what does any of that have to do with us and the water?«
»Again, perfectly simple,« replied Ben. »We're telling you to turn the city water supply on again at midnight. If you don't, we'll start making your gang disappear. One by one, to give you time to **reconsider**. We're not monsters. Let's say . . .« – here Ben paused briefly, acted as if he were thinking off the top of his head, glanced around, and looked hard at each of the bodyguards. Then he allowed his gaze to move to the porter's lodge, and spoke again.
»Let's say we start with your friend in the porter's lodge there. Siggi, isn't it? Yes, good idea: if we don't get the water back at midnight we'll make Siggi disappear! It's up to you, Kolya.«

(to) cast a glance at sb/sth: einen Blick werfen auf jdn/etw

(to) reconsider: noch einmal überdenken

blackmail: die Erpressung

Kolya was stunned. Somehow he'd lost control of the situation. *He* had made the demands. *He* was the one in control of the water, and he meant to use it as a **blackmail** tool. And now, suddenly, things seemed to be the other way around!

»You're crazy!« he shouted through the gate. »Who says you can really do it? I don't believe for a moment you can make people disappear.«

»Too bad. Don't, then!« replied Jennifer, shrugging. Ben understood at once and went on bluffing.

»She's right,« he said. »No one can force you to believe us. You'll just have to wait and see. We'll be back tomorrow.«

Frank, too, saw that their plan was working out. This was the time to go away and leave Kolya alone with his uncertainty about their powers. It would cause a certain amount of confusion in the gang's camp.

»See you, then, Kolya. If I were you I really would turn the water on again. But it's up to you.« And Frank began to walk away again. Ben and Jennifer joined him.

»Stop!« called Kolya suddenly. Ben, Jennifer and Frank turned round.

grating: das Gitter

»I have a much better idea,« said Kolya, and looked at his bodyguards. »Get them!« he ordered. The guards raced forward at once, jumped up on the **grating** of the gate and clambered over it.

»Quick, run!« Frank, Ben and Jennifer ran as fast as they could. The first two bodyguards followed about a hundred metres behind. Running was no problem for that keen sportsman Frank, and Jennifer had no trouble in increasing her lead on their pursuers either. She was the second fastest girl in her class. But Ben was gasping and panting as he followed. Running had never been his strong point. Frank stopped.

»You go on,« he called to Jennifer. Then he turned and waited for Ben. He **scanned** their surroundings, without spotting anything that could help Ben. There was a bike leaning against a wall a little way off, but it was padlocked. And the bodyguards were getting alarmingly close.

(to) scan: mit Blicken absuchen

»Here, turn right!« Frank shouted to Ben.

They ran down a small side street on their right. »How about Jennifer?« gasped Ben.

»Don't worry about her,« Frank said hastily. »She's a good sprinter.«

Ben realized that he was the problem. »Sorry, I just can't go any faster,« he **panted**.

(to) pant: keuchen

»That's okay,« said Frank, »but you must keep going. This way!«

The two of them ran down the next side street to the left, and the next on the right after that. »Where are we?« asked Ben as they went along.

»No idea,« said Frank, »but we have to get out of sight of those bodyguards. Our only chance of shaking them off is if they have to search for us. In here!«

Frank and Ben ran inside the entrance of a building.

»I have an idea!« gasped Ben. »Leave the door open.«
»Are you crazy?« Frank was horrified. »But then they'll see right away we ran in here.«
»That's the point,« Ben said, pressing a red button to call the lift. They were standing right in front of it. »I hope it works. Too bad for us if it doesn't.«
»What are you planning?« asked Frank.
»Take a look outside and see if you can spot the bodyguards yet,« said Ben briefly. »Tell me when they come around the corner. It's okay if they see you.«
Frank felt bad. So Ben had a plan – but Frank hoped he hadn't miscalculated. However, this was not the moment to argue. Frank did as Ben had told him and looked out of the door of the building into the side street. By now the lift had arrived. Ben opened its door and pressed the button for the top floor – the eighth. He came out of the lift again but held the door open.
»It works with a lot of lifts,« said Ben. »Let's hope it does with this one!«
Frank had no time to answer. »They're coming!« he shouted. »And they've seen me.«
»Good – then let's get down to the cellar,« said Ben, who had seen that the door to the cellar wasn't locked. He let the lift door close and followed Frank down into the cellar. As soon as he'd closed the cellar door behind them he heard the empty lift going up to the top floor as the bodyguards rushed into the

hall. Ben was pleased. **Jerking his thumb up**, he showed Frank that his plan was working, though in the dark Frank couldn't see it.

»Hey, they've gone up on the lift,« one of the bodyguards called. Ben heard him from behind the cellar door. At last Frank saw Ben's plan. Ben tried to locate Frank's ear in the dark, went as close to him as possible and whispered, »How many?« Frank **caught on** at once, and knew Ben meant the bodyguards. He took Ben's right hand and silently counted the fingers on it with his own hands. Ben understood; five bodyguards.

»Come on, up the stairs. Now we've got them!« called another bodyguard. And soon all five of them were running upstairs. Ben put his ear to the cellar door and listened **intently**.

»One of us ought to stay down at the bottom,« Ben heard someone say, but a good deal further off this time. They must all be up on the first floor by now.

»Okay, Pete and I will go down again!«

»No, only one of you. That'll do.«

This was their chance!

»Now – quick!« Ben whispered to Frank, and he opened the cellar door as quietly as possible. The two of them tiptoed out of the cellar, through the front door of the building and into the street as they heard the loud footsteps of the bodyguards on the stairs coming down again.

»Okay – off we go!« said Ben, still in a whisper, and

(to) jerk one´s thumb up: den Daumen hochhalten

(to) catch on: kapieren

intently: aufmerksam, **konzentriert, forschend**

next moment both boys were running as fast as they could go back to the street corner. They retraced their route in the opposite direction: first side street on the left, then right, and then they were back in the main road where they had parted from Jennifer.

»Come on,« said Ben. »They'll probably still be looking for us in that building, but you never know.«

appreciatively: anerkennend

»Not a bad trick!« said Frank **appreciatively**. »And now let's get back to the school!«

Frank and Ben found a large number of children there already. About fifty of them, Ben guessed, all standing around in the yard wanting to know what was up in the city. They had come in response to the loudspeaker announcements by Miriam, Norbert, Martin and Christopher. Thomas and Miriam were standing on a shed roof – just as Ben had done four days ago – trying to explain the situation to the new arrivals through an old megaphone they had found in the school cellar. Several other children were busy making supper in the small hall. They couldn't cook noodles this evening because there wasn't any water, but luckily Martin had thought of that while driving around, and had brought back two hundred cans of ravioli in sauce.

Half an hour later, a hundred and thirty children were sitting happily in the small hall, eating steaming hot ravioli.

All the same, there was a mood of nervous tension.

Was Ben right? Would Siggi really disappear at midnight? And even if he did, would Kolya fall for the trick and turn the water on again? The children were asking themselves these questions all over the hall.

Frank had a second **helping** of ravioli. »Maybe we ought to send someone to the waterworks to keep watch in secret and see what happens?« he heard Jennifer say as he went back to his table.

»Good idea!« said Miriam. »Jennifer, we could both go.« Jennifer agreed, and the other children thought it a good **notion**, too, so it was **settled**.

At ten in the evening, the two girls put the things they might need most into a backpack: a walkie-talkie radio, two torches, **a pair of binoculars** from the biology lab, some sandwiches and a bottle of sparkling water. Then they set off.

They were in luck: when they reached the waterworks they saw that Siggi was still sitting in the porter's lodge – or if he'd left it then he was back again. Jennifer and Miriam sat on a bench near the bus stop – right opposite the main entrance to the waterworks. This was a good, convenient observation post, because the bus stop wasn't lit – nor were any others in town at the moment. From here they had a good view of the porter's lodge with the light on in it, but they couldn't be seen themselves.

Miriam opened the backpack and took out a sandwich. »I'm so excited I'm hungry again,« she said, taking a good bite out of it.

helping: die Portion

notion: die Idee
to settle: abmachen, festlegen

a pair of binoculars: das Fernglas

»Well, I had three helpings of ravioli, so I'm really full. I think you can eat all the sandwiches we brought,« said Jennifer.

(to) munch: mampfen

Miriam **munched** her sandwich while Jennifer looked up at the stars in the clear, dark sky. Nothing was happening in the porter's lodge opposite or on the forecourt of the waterworks. Jennifer looked at her watch: it was quarter to eleven. They had over an hour to wait to find out if Ben's plan was going to work.

After a short pause, Miriam asked, »Hey, Jennifer, is there anything between you and Ben?«

»Oh, I don't know,« said Jennifer. When she and Miriam were alone they could discuss such subjects freely. »I mean, I really like Ben. Maybe I wouldn't mind going out with him either. But I guess he doesn't feel the same way.«

»Why don't you just tell him?« suggested Miriam. She had always been more direct than Jennifer in such matters.

»I can't,« said Jennifer at once. »Either Ben will realize I'd like to go out with him or he won't. If he doesn't notice for himself there's no point in it.«

»I don't think so at all,« objected Miriam. »With my last two boyfriends, well, it was like this, I . . .«

(to) get around to sth: zu etwas kommen

But Miriam never **got around to** finishing her story.

»Look!« called Jennifer. Two boys were walking over the forecourt of the waterworks to the porter's lodge. One of them had a small packet in his hand.

The other was searching his trouser pocket for something. They stopped outside the door of the lodge.
Miriam snatched the binoculars out of the backpack to take a closer look. »Oh wow!« she said, after a moment.
Jennifer didn't understand. She moved to take the binoculars herself and see what had surprised Miriam so much. But Miriam waved her back. »Just a moment,« she said in excitement, without lowering the binoculars. »They've locked him in!«
Jennifer didn't understand. Miriam handed her the binoculars and repeated what she had seen.
»Siggi's not on watch in the porter's lodge – they're keeping him prisoner there,« said the excited Miriam.
Looking through the binoculars, Jennifer realized that Miriam was right. »So they are,« she said, puzzled. »What does *that* mean?«
The two boys left the porter's lodge again, locked the door carefully behind them, and **retraced their steps** over the forecourt. They had given Siggi the packet.
»They were taking him something to eat,« said Jennifer. She put the binoculars down on the bench. »I guess Kolya wants to find out if we were telling the truth. He won't turn the water on, he's going to let Siggi stew in there and see if he disappears at midnight or not.«

(to) retrace one's steps: auf demselben Weg zurückgehen (auf dem man gekommen ist)

guinea pig: das Meerschweinchen, hier: Versuchskaninchen

»And I don't suppose Siggi was happy to be Kolya's **guinea pig,**« finished Miriam. »He's not the bravest person I ever met anyway. I bet they had a quarrel, and then Kolya simply locked Siggi in so he won't run away.«

Jennifer took out the walkie-talkie and reported back to HQ on what they'd seen. Thomas and Ben, sitting by the central walkie-talkie at school, thought Miriam's and Jennifer's assessment of the situation made sense.

»Poor old Siggi,« remarked Ben. »He must be feeling bad. Wondering whether he'll disappear or not! And of course he doesn't know.«

Miriam looked at the time: twenty past eleven. »We'll soon know if you're right, Ben,« she said.

»I'm assuming it will be the way I suspected and Siggi will vanish at midnight,« said Ben over the radio.

»What if he doesn't?« asked Jennifer.

»No idea!« said Ben.

For if he didn't they'd have to think of some other way of getting the water back. *But what?*

A Tricky Situation

At two minutes before midnight the forecourt of the waterworks got very crowded. Kolya and a whole bunch of kids went to the porter's lodge. Jennifer thought there must be about fifty of them, although only ten were girls, as far as she could see from this distance at first glance. Siggi was still sitting in the little **glazed** lodge, running both hands desperately through his hair. His watch was on the desk in front of him, and he kept on looking at it. Miriam could see everything through the binoculars.

glazed: verglast

»He's crying,« said Miriam.

»I'm not surprised,« remarked Jennifer. »Look at that bunch! Fifty of them standing staring to see if Siggi is going to disappear or not. I call that horrible.«

»You can say that again,« agreed Miriam, who felt sorry for Siggi now.

»Not that we're really much better,« commented Jennifer.

Miriam lowered the binoculars and turned to look at her friend. »It's not the same,« she said indignantly.« We're keeping watch on our enemies who've turned off the whole city's water supply. It's not our fault if they've shut Siggi up!«

»Yes, you're right,« agreed Jennifer.

»How late is it now?« asked Miriam, looking through the binoculars again.

Jennifer looked at the time.

»Seven minutes past twelve,« she said, reading the face of her watch.

»Are you sure your watch is working?« asked Miriam suspiciously. Jennifer assured her that it was.

Miriam put the binoculars down on her **lap** again.

lap: der Schoß

»But Siggi's still there,« she said. »According to Ben's

despondently: niedergeschlagen, mutlos, bedrückt
(to) mill around: umherlaufen

theory he ought to have disappeared long ago – if your watch is keeping good time.«

Jennifer picked up the walkie-talkie and reported the news to HQ. Ben was there on the receiving end.

»I don't understand it,« he muttered **despondently**. A hundred and thirty children were **milling around** him – of course they couldn't all fit into the school office, so they were crowded together in the corridor of the school administration building. They looked disappointed. Ben's plan had sounded so brilliant; they'd already been celebrating victory over Kolya the night before. Was everything going wrong now?

»Kolya's picking up the phone,« Miriam announced.

»And I know who he's calling,« said Ben a moment later. »The phone here is ringing.«

Frank went to the phone in the school office. Ben held the walkie-talkie close to the earpiece and pressed the Send button, so that Jennifer and Miriam could hear the telephone conversation, too.

»Hello, is that Frank? How about your magic tricks now? Siggi's still with us!« called Kolya over the phone.

Frank said nothing. Kolya went on. »Well, nothing to say? Ha, ha, I bet you don't! Talking so big and all! Let me tell you again: I'm the real boss of this city, and there won't be any water until you get that into your heads!«

Click.

Kolya had ended his call.
There was a lot of shouting and laughing in the porter's lodge. Kolya's fifty gang members were yelling and applauding. Those still out on the forecourt shot several flares into the air with their pistols.
»Did you hear all that?« asked Ben over the radio, gloomily.
»Yes,« said Jennifer. »Guess what's going on here!«
She described Kolya's wild celebrations. She and Miriam could see them from their bench. What with first their excitement and then their disappointment, the two girls didn't realize that they could now be seen clearly from the waterworks forecourt in the light of the red and green flares. When they did realize, it was too late. They couldn't imagine where the boys had come from so fast, but suddenly they were surrounded by ten members of the gang.
»Well, well, who have we here?« smirked one of them. »Aren't these the chicks who go around with Ben and Frank?«
Another boy confirmed it.
»Won't Kolya just be pleased!« said the first boy, grabbing Miriam's arm roughly. He pulled her up from the bench and was going to drag her over the street to the waterworks, but Miriam gave him a hefty kick on the **shin**. The boy yelped and limped off on one leg.
»Don't you dare touch me, you disgusting horror!« Miriam spat after him.

shin: das Schienbein

Two other boys fell on Miriam and held her by both arms. »Come with us!« they shouted.
Jennifer jumped up from the bench. »Let her go!« she protested, but two more boys had already pushed in between her and the captive Miriam.
»Not a hope,« said a fat boy with a shaven head and a baseball cap, standing right in front of Jennifer and grinning nastily at her. »There's no point. Be a good girl and come along. I don't hit girls,« he added, **with a grand gesture**.

with a grand gesture: mit großmütiger Geste

»How sensible of you,« said Jennifer. »I hit boys, though!« No sooner had she spoken than she hit the fat boy on the head with the backpack, which still had the bottle of sparkling water in it. The fat boy yelled, fell forward and put both hands to his head. Something warm ran over them.
»I'm bleeding!« he cried. »My head is bleeding!«
For a moment the other boys stood there **rooted to the spot**, looking in horror at their companion. Jennifer took her chance. She jumped over the bench, right into the gap left by the two boys when they **hauled** Miriam **away**. As Jennifer landed she almost **stumbled**, but she managed to regain her balance just in time. Then she ran faster than she had ever run in her life before, or that's what it felt like anyway. Three of the ten boys immediately took off after her.
»Run, Jennifer, run! You can make it!« shouted Miriam after her.

(to) be rooted to the spot: wie angewurzelt dastehen

(to) haul away: mit aller Kraft davonzerren

(to) stumble: stolpern

»Shut up!« one of her guards ordered, twisting her right arm so hard that she almost screamed. But she wasn't going to show weakness in front of the gang. She bravely clenched her teeth and kept back the cry of pain. Instead of screaming, she told the boy who had hurt her, »Jennifer's the second fastest girl sprinter in our class. You'll never catch her!«
The boy briefly turned his head to see for himself how fast Jennifer was running. In that fraction of a second when he wasn't paying attention Miriam pulled her right hand free and scratched her second guard with her fingernails, raking them across his face so that he yelled and held his bleeding nose. Like a flash, Miriam turned and kicked the first boy hard on the shin just as he was about to grab her again. He yelled, too, withdrew his leg and hopped around his friend in a circle. Miriam made a break for it at once. But she stood no chance. There were still five other boys, grabbing her arms and pulling her hair. Miriam yelled, kicked and bit like a mad dog. The boys **swerved**, flinched back and made sure their hands were safe. But just as Miriam freed herself from one boy there was always another to grab her. Even she, hissing and hitting out, had no chance against five boys at once. They dragged her into the porter's lodge where Siggi had still been locked a few minutes ago. Now he was out on the forecourt, with the forty other boys and girls still yelling and shouting triumphantly around him. Kolya gave Siggi a friendly slap on the back.

(to) swerve: einen Bogen machen, ausweichen

(to) **boast**: prahlen, angeben

»Just like I said,« Miriam heard Kolya **boast**. »They can't make anyone disappear.«

But Siggi was looking darkly at Kolya. »No need to carry on like that,« he said angrily. »You weren't sure. And you were ready to let them try it on me. Go away!«

distinct: deutlich
quiver: das Zittern

Miriam noticed a **distinct quiver** in Siggi's voice. He wasn't far from tears again, she thought. Kolya didn't miss Siggi's trembling voice either.

»Oho!« said Kolya. »Listen to him, will you! Now he's cross because I saw through the plan Frank and Ben **had hatched up** – what a useless couple! But you just remember this, you **washout**,« he said, looking hard at Siggi. »Kolya doesn't give up – certainly not for a coward like you!«

(to) **hatch up**: ausbrüten
washout: die Flasche, die Niete

That did it; Siggi began to cry. The other boys laughed at him. »Hey, look at him! Crying like a girlie!«

Hearing that made Miriam furious. *Crying like a girlie! What does he mean by that?* she thought. *Just a moment ago I kicked two boys' shins and scratched another's nose, it took five of them to overpower me, and they say a thing like that! Typical boys, always thinking they're so marvellous!* Miriam noticed the door of the porter's lodge being locked after her. She turned and stuck her tongue out at her guards. »You **jerks**!« she shouted. »Stupid jerks, that's you!«

jerk: der Trottel

Jennifer had run as only she could. This was the second time she'd been **scarpering** from Kolya's thugs. *I*

(to) **scarper**: türmen, fliehen

must be doing something wrong, thought Jennifer, *I always have these characters after me!* But yet again she got safely away, although she didn't have such a good start as before. After a few hundred metres, however, Kolya's supporters had abandoned the chase, out of breath. Jennifer would never have guessed her ability to run fast would come in so useful. Her sports teacher was always pleased with her when they had matches against other sports clubs, but she herself never thought much of the certificates she brought home. They weren't very well designed, she thought. But now, for the first time in her life, Jennifer was **genuinely** glad to be such a fast sprinter.

genuinely: wirklich

She arrived at the school out of breath, ran across the school yard and burst into the school office. Ben, Frank, Thomas and the others looked up in alarm. They were still standing around the walkie-talkie, calling again and again. »Jennifer! Miriam! Report in! What's happened?«

»What are you doing here?« asked Ben, the first to recover from his shock.« Where's Miriam? Why aren't you two still at the waterworks?«

»Give me a moment!« gasped Jennifer. She took a few deep breaths and then, exhausted, dropped into a chair that Frank had immediately vacated for her. In a **hesitant, agitated** voice she began to tell her tale. When Jennifer had finished, there was **dismal** silence in the school office.

hesitant: hier: stockend
agitated: aufgeregt
dismal: bedrückt, betreten

»Your plan didn't work, Ben,« said Frank. »Something went wrong. Life in the city isn't following the rules of the computer game after all.«
Ben shook his head. He could think of no reply. He didn't have any explanation for why Siggi hadn't disappeared either – and yet something inside him told him he was right. He simply must be right. Because if he wasn't it meant that their life in this city really wasn't going by the rules of the game. And only if it did would they reach Level Four and get the grown-ups back. There must be some logical explanation for Siggi's failure to disappear, and Ben knew he must find out what it was if he wasn't to **destroy** all their hopes. He felt a heavy responsibility weighing him down. His passion for computers was suddenly deadly serious, and now he had to use all he knew about them for everyone's good. Ben took a deep breath – and decided to keep his thoughts to himself.

(to) destroy: zerstören

»Where's the walkie-talkie?« asked Norbert at last.
Jennifer shrugged her shoulders. »No idea. Either they've taken it away from Miriam or it's still on the bench where we were sitting.«
Norbert frowned. »That means,« he said, »we must assume that Kolya can listen in to our conversations over the radio now – or at least the ones that go out to all groups.« He turned to Thomas. »So you'd better radio the groups separately, Thomas. No general calls!«

»I thought of that long ago,« replied Thomas. »I'm just wondering, what do we do now? Kolya is still in control of the **water supply**, and now he has Miriam, too. The situation's worse than it was this morning. Can anyone tell me what we're going to do?«

»Don't start **whinging** again,« snapped Ben. Thomas's habit of looking on the dark side was getting him down. »Let's get some sleep. It's two in the morning. And tomorrow we'll all need clear heads to make new plans.«

»Good idea,« agreed Frank. »We can't do anything for Miriam today anyway.« He helped the exhausted Jennifer up from her chair and was about to leave the school office with her. But at that moment the phone rang.

Frank and Jennifer froze. The others stared at the telephone, too. It could only be Kolya! This was too much for Ben. He jumped up, snatched the phone and shouted into the mouthpiece, »I've had about enough of you, you great **Barbary ape**! Let Miriam go and turn the water back on! Who do you think you are?«

»I always thought I was Miriam,« said a voice the other end of the phone.

»Miriam!« Ben **positively squawked** her name into the receiver in surprise. All the others immediately came crowding round, pressing close so that they could hear Miriam over the phone, too. Ben was still shouting. »Miriam, where are you? What are you doing? Where's Kolya?«

water supply: die Wasserversorgung

(to) whinge: jammern, meckern, plärren

Barbary ape: der Berberaffe; hier im Sinne von »Affenarsch«

positively: hier: wirklich, echt

(to) squawk: kreischen

»Shut up a minute, will you, or you'll never know,« said Miriam.

Ben abruptly closed his mouth.

»Did Jennifer get back to you all right?« asked Miriam.

»I'm fine!« called Jennifer from behind Ben.

»Great!« said Miriam, relieved. She went on. »I'm not as fast as Jennifer, I'm afraid, that's why they caught me. But I laid into them. Two have bruised shins – I think one of them's still limping – and another has a nasty scratch on his nose. He won't want to go into a disco with visual security controls in a hurry.«

»Terrific,« Jennifer called again, but Ben signed to her to be quiet.

»That's good, Miriam, but you can tell us all your stories later. Where are you? What's happened to you?«

»What do you mean, stories?« protested Miriam. »I'm telling you the facts.«

»Yes, yes, we believe you,« Ben soothed her, impatiently. »Go on!«

»Okay,« said Miriam. »Well, I'm a prisoner. In the porter's lodge, like Siggi earlier. But they were **crowing** so hard over Siggi still being here they quite forgot there's a phone in the porter's lodge. And I'd written the school's number on my hand. So half an hour ago they all went back into the red brick building – except for Siggi. He's furious because Kolya was ready to sacrifice him. So he stayed outside, **sulking**. Right here outside the porter's lodge.«

(to) crow: jauchzen

(to) sulk: schmollen

»And can he hear everything you're saying over the phone at the moment?« Ben interrupted.
»No, he can't!« replied Miriam instantly. »That's really why I'm calling. Siggi has disappeared!«
Ben held his breath for a moment. Then he asked, »What do you mean, *Siggi has disappeared*?«
»Well, like I say, disappeared! He suddenly wasn't there. One moment he was, the next he wasn't. I was sitting here. I was watching him muttering angrily to himself. And then he was suddenly gone!«
»Why didn't you say so before? When was this?« Ben asked.
»What do you mean, why didn't I say so before? You**'re not letting me get a word in edgeways**,« Miriam protested. »It was about ten minutes ago.«
»But that means our plan worked! Siggi disappeared after all. Just like I said,« cried Ben, delighted. The heavy burden of responsibility was lifted from his shoulders. He'd known it! Everything *was* working by the rules of the game!
»That's right,« agreed Miriam. »The only trouble is that it happened two hours too late. No one saw. Except me.«
Ben thought that over.
»What's up? Ben! Are you still there?« said Miriam.
Frank took the phone from Ben's hand. »Yes, we're still here, Miriam. Do you have time to talk to us without being interrupted?« he asked.
Miriam said yes.

not to let sb get a word in edgeways: jdn nicht zu Wort kommen lassen

»Listen,« Frank went on. »Hide that phone after we ring off, if you can. If Kolya's gang don't see it, maybe they won't remember it. We won't call you, but you can always call us when you're on your own. Don't worry, Miriam! We'll soon have you out of there!«
»I should just about think so!« replied Miriam. »You're not going to leave me where I am, I hope!«
»I know!« cried Ben suddenly, reaching for the phone. »I know why Siggi was so late disappearing,« he explained, speaking into the phone and looking at the other children around him in the school office. »It's because computers work very precisely. All the people in the game disappear at the end of their fifteenth year of life. But Siggi probably wasn't born at midnight on the dot – it looks like he was born at one forty-five in the morning! So his fifteenth year of life wasn't over until one forty-five, and that's why he didn't disappear till then. Why didn't it occur to me before?«
»I wish it had,« said Miriam over the phone. »Because then our plan would have worked and I wouldn't be a prisoner here.«
»Look, I'm really sorry,« Ben told her. »But it does prove my theory right: everything's following the rules of the computer game.«
»And what use is that to us now?« asked Miriam. »I've no idea if any of the rest of the gang are going to have a birthday tomorrow or the day after.«
»I don't know what use it is to us *yet*«, Ben told her.

»But it's still an advantage, one in our favour and not Kolya's. And we'll **exploit** it. You bet we will, Miriam, and we'll have you out of there tomorrow!«

(to) exploit: ausnutzen

If only I knew how, thought Ben, but he kept that to himself. He simply had to think of something. He had to!

He ended the phone conversation with Miriam and rang off.

That night he crept into his sleeping bag very thoughtfully. Even when the quiet breathing and faint snores of the other hundred and thirty children could be heard in the gym, Ben still lay awake for a long, long time, thinking.

There must be some solution, thought Ben, feeling the weight of responsibility come back. He had to carry it for all of them because of his knowledge of computers. He couldn't escape it. He was the one, the only one who must think what to do next. *There must be some solution* . . . And finally Ben fell asleep too.

Ben Has an Idea

»Got it!« Ben **woke with a start**. It wasn't even six in the morning yet, but he was suddenly wide awake. While he was still half asleep an idea had come into his head out of the blue. *Everything that happens follows the rules of the computer game!* Ben had gone to bed with that idea, had fallen asleep with it, and yet it

(to) wake with a start: aus dem Schlaf hochschrecken

(to) summon up: heraufbeschwören

(to) outwit: austricksen, überlisten

hadn't told him very much. However, now it was perfectly clear. *Like the computer game*! He had only to play the computer game all the way through again in his head – or at least as far as he knew it. Ben **summoned up** the whole game before his mind's eye. *First you see the city, with the cars driving around. You have to go along the street. Watch out for that flower pot! A flower pot falls out of a window. You have to jump aside*. No, that bit wasn't important now. *What next? Oh yes, you have to go into the shop. The salesman isn't really a salesman, he's a magician. The key is in the glass case. You have to get it*. And then Ben remembered the error that kept coming up in the game just where the whole mess they were now in began: the magician had suddenly disappeared, although he wasn't supposed to. *Of course!* Why hadn't he thought of it before?

»That's it!« cried Ben. »That's the way we'll **outwit** Kolya!«

Frank and Jennifer, who were sleeping near Ben, woke with a start.

»What's the matter?« asked Jennifer, looking around her, drowsy and confused. Frank looked round the gym too, but all he could see was the sleeping children.

»Are you crazy or what?« he asked Ben.

Ben ignored the question. He crawled over to Frank and Jennifer. »I know how we can fool Kolya and rescue Miriam!« he whispered. He didn't want to wake more of the children. He hadn't worked out his idea well enough to tell it to **all and sundry** just yet, not after the failure of his first plan. So he said softly, »You remember the computer game?«

all and sundry: jedermann

Jennifer fell back in her sleeping bag and buried her head in her pillow. *Oh no, not that computer game again!*

Ben stuck to his point. »Frank, you know the game, too!«

Frank nodded slowly.

»I spent all night thinking about it. How it all began and so on. And then I remembered the bit with the magician.«

»What magician?« asked Jennifer.

Ben explained about that part of the game. »So you have to reach the glass case in the shop, because it has the key to the next room in it. But first you have to outwit the magician.«

»So?« Jennifer interrupted him. »Are we about to play computer games now or what? At six in the morning?«

»Wait a minute, do!« Ben said impatiently. »You have to be very careful in your **battle of wits** with the magician on the way to the glass case. Because there's a trapdoor in the middle of the shop. It leads down into a huge labyrinth, and once you're in it – well, **it's curtains for you!**«

a battle of wits: ein geistiges Kräftemessen

it's curtains for you!: hier sinngemäß: na, dann Gute Nacht!

Jennifer groaned. »Oh, for goodness' sake, Ben, come to the point! I'm tired to death,« she wailed.

»Everything that happens to us follows the rules of

the computer game,« Ben repeated his theory. »We've seen that. And last night with Siggi was the final proof of it.«

»So now you think there's a magician wandering about town?« said Jennifer sarcastically.

Ben took her question seriously. »No,« he replied. »He'd be an adult and too old, so that can't be it.«

»But . . . ?« said Frank.

»But the trapdoor!« said Ben, beaming. »If everything works the same as in the computer game, then there must be a shop here where we'll find that trapdoor leading to the labyrinth!«

twaddle: dummes Geschätz, hier: So ein Quatsch!

»**Twaddle**!« said Jennifer crossly. »The computer game shows some kind of imaginary city, not ours. Nothing here has changed. All the buildings and shops are the way they always were.«

»There's one little detail you're overlooking, Jennifer,« Ben insisted. »The city in the computer game is only shown on a kind of **schematic grid**. All the buildings are just **symbolic boxes**. That's why they can take any shape. Or to put it another way, they don't change *our* buildings, but they can change certain functions of them.«

schematic grid: das schematische System
symbolic box: hier: der symbolhafte Kasten

»I don't get it,« Frank complained.

»I mean,« Ben went on, »a shop in our city stays the same shop. But inside it you might suddenly find that trapdoor. A cellar that never used to be anything but a cellar could suddenly have turned into a labyrinth. Without any sign of it on the outside.«

»What you're saying sounds kind of weird,« said Jennifer.
»Well, we've been right in the middle of a weird adventure for the last few days, right?« replied Ben.
»But things like that don't happen. You mean a labyrinth would just suddenly **pop up** here somewhere?« Jennifer still couldn't really believe it.
But Ben was feeling more and more sure of himself. »A few days ago we wouldn't have believed all the grown-ups could just disappear either. But they did.«
Yes, they definitely had. Even Jennifer couldn't **quibble about** that. And anyway, if there was a chance of freeing Miriam, no matter how small a chance, they had to take it.
»So you want **to lure** Kolya into falling through this trapdoor?« asked Jennifer, to make sure she had it straight. Ben nodded.
»But how are we going to do that? Why would Kolya come to the shop?« Jennifer went on.
Ben had thought about that problem already. »We tell him we'll go along with his condition and accept him as boss of the city. In return he must turn the water on again and set Miriam free. And we'll get him to come to the shop with the trapdoor in it for – let's say for official negotiations.«
Jennifer doubted whether Kolya would go along with that, but it could wait. Something else was more important for now. »Where is this shop anyway?« she asked.

(to) pop up: auftauchen

(to) quibble about: (an etw.) deuteln

(to) lure: anlocken, ködern

»Well, that's the problem,« Ben admitted. »We'll have to look for it.«

steeply: steil

»Look for it?« Frank's eyebrows rose **steeply**. »You mean we have to search every shop in town for a trapdoor?« He very much hoped he'd misunderstood Ben's plan, because searching all the shops would take days. Ben, however, had meant just that.

»Only it's not the actual trapdoor we're looking for but a glass case with a key in it,« Ben explained. »We won't be able to see the trapdoor.«

Frank heaved a deep sigh. Look for a glass case? How were they going to do that?

(to) quell: niederschlagen, zerschlagen, bändigen

Ben read Frank's mind. »There's over a hundred of us,« he said, trying to **quell** his friend's doubts. »We can hope it won't be the very last shop we look at. If we concentrate hard, it ought to be possible to do the search in half a day.«

(to) object: einwenden, entgegnen

»I can see another problem, too,« Frank **objected**. »We don't really know a lot of these hundred and thirty kids well. I don't know if we can trust them all. If just one of them decides to give our plan away to Kolya, we can pack it in.«

Ben nodded. He, too, feared the same thing.

»We must think of some excuse not to tell everyone about it,« suggested Frank.

(to) go into a huddle: die Köpfe zusammenstecken

»No,« said Jennifer. »Up till now we've all done everything together, and I'd say we've solved our problems that way. We don't want **to go into a huddle** now, making secret plans and getting other people to run around doing the **donkey work** for us. I don't think that's right.«

donkey work: die Dreckarbeit

»But there's too much risk,« said Ben. »We're not sure if everyone will really back us up, and this plan is too important for us to endanger it.«

»I think so, too,« Frank agreed. »Sometimes one person has to decide.«

»Sometimes one person has to decide!« repeated Jennifer, wrinkling her nose. »You know, that's exactly what Kolya said, too.« Jennifer felt anger rising in her. *All boys are the same*, she thought crossly. *Given half a chance they want to make the decisions, or show how tough they are, like Frank outside the waterworks when he nearly got into a fight with Kolya.*

Jennifer took a deep breath to control her anger. She tried to speak calmly, which made her voice shake slightly. »If I've got the right idea about your silly computer game, then there are points to be won for getting as many as possible of the kids in the city together so we can solve the problems *by co-operating with each other*. And if you trick the kids or cheat them, surely points get deducted – that's to say if there's any logic in this lousy game at all.«

Ben and Frank looked at each other, wide-eyed: it was a fact! There were several places in the game which did work that way – or at least much that way. If the community lost any kids, you lost points, too.

Jennifer saw that she was getting somewhere. »And if everything in this city is following the rules of your wretched computer game like you said, Ben . . .« Jennifer spoke so sharply that Ben flinched slightly . . . »well, in that case we won't solve the city's problems by not telling the other kids our plans!«

Ben and Frank were speechless. Jennifer had read them quite a lecture, and she was right! That was exactly the principle of the game, and Ben, the outstanding mathematician and computer specialist, hadn't thought of it. It had taken Jennifer to explain the logical rules of the game to him. In a way she'd beaten him with his own weapons, because it had been Ben's idea that the city worked by the rules of the computer game.

Ben cleared his throat, feeling awkward. *She's right*, he thought. He knew she was.

Jennifer was indeed right, even more so than she knew just at that moment. Because Ben realized that he didn't always have to find the brilliant solution for himself – even if he was a computer wizard. Jennifer had just shown him, very clearly, that other kids could understand the situation, too, and develop it further. He felt glad he wouldn't always have to do all the thinking about the game on his own. But he had a funny feeling inside him, too, wondering if he hadn't often underestimated people who weren't necessarily maths geniuses in the past. Had he sometimes put them down in a **lofty** manner?

lofty: stolz, hochmütig

Frank was thoughtfully scratching his head. Jennifer stood up.

»Where are you going?« Frank asked her.
»We've just made a plan,« Jennifer replied firmly. »So now we must get ready for a meeting. Wake the others up and tell them. We'll start in half an hour.«
Once again Jennifer had taken over very efficiently.
Three quarters of an hour later, Jennifer was telling the meeting of all the children about Ben's idea. Opinions were divided. Some, like Thomas and Norbert, were ready to put the new plan into action at once. They were keen to teach Kolya a lesson and get the water running again. Others were very sceptical. But though they **racked their brains**, they couldn't think of any better idea, so in the end they agreed to Jennifer's suggestion.
The children divided up quickly into small groups to set out in search of a shop with a glass case in it. And there had to be a key in the case.
»Stop – wait a minute!« called Ben, as the first groups were almost out of the door. »You must be very, very careful, because the trapdoor will be invisible. So take a close look around the glass case, but don't run wild in the shop. And there's one more thing: it'll probably be a very small one. No need to go searching the big department stores.«
The children **scattered** in all directions, with Ben's warning in mind. Thomas stayed at HQ with the walkie-talkie radio again. This time, however, he also had to answer the phone. The children had divided into so many groups that there weren't nearly enough

(to) rack one`s brains: sich den Kopf/das Hirn zermartern

(to) scatter: verstreuen

(to) recruite: anstellen, einstellen
switchboard: die Telefonzentrale
operator: die Vermittlung
(to) man: besetzen (Büro, Posten, Kontrollpunkt), bedienen (Telefon)

radios to go round, so a number of the groups would be phoning in with the results of their searches instead. But never mind – Thomas had **recruited** a useful **switchboard operator**. Little Max was keen to **man** the phone, and Thomas was glad of his help. Too much rushing around wasn't his idea of a good time, and you might, thought Thomas, have to rush around a lot if you were in charge of two means of communication.

Thomas and Max waited by the phone and the radio for a good hour, but nothing happened. Max was getting impatient, sitting on a chair swinging his legs and feeling bored. He caught the rays of the sun coming through the window in a magnifying glass, and shone the concentrated sunbeam on the headmaster's desk.

»Hey, Max, don't set the whole place alight,« Thomas warned as smoke began to rise from the desk. Max was about to answer back when the phone rang. Max jumped up, snatched the phone off the hook and answered it. »This is the good kids' HQ. Max here.«

Thomas grinned at him.

»Hi, Max,« said a voice the other end. »What are *you* doing there? It's Miriam. Anyone else with you?«

»They're all out looking for a trapdoor so that Kolya can fall down it, and then you'll be rescued,« Max told her.

Miriam couldn't make much of this. Thomas took the phone from Max.

»It's Miriam calling from the bad kids' HQ,« Max told him mysteriously. Thomas nodded.
»Hi, Miriam. How are you?« he asked.
»Okay. What's Max going on about?«
Thomas explained the plan. Meanwhile the radio beeped. Max jumped up and pressed the right button.
»HQ here . . .« But he was interrupted.
»We've found it!« shouted Martin over the radio. »We've located the glass case!«
Max dropped the radio on the floor, ran over to Thomas, **tugged** his pullover and shouted, »They've found it! They've tracked the glass case down!«

(to) tug: zerren, ziehen

Thomas said goodbye to Miriam, crawled over to the walkie-talkie radio in slow motion – or that's how it seemed to Max – slowly picked it up, and asked, »Where?« Then he made a note. *The hairdresser's in Little Garden Street. Norbert's group.*
»Right,« he said. »Stay there. I'll send the others round to you.«
The phone was already ringing again. Max said his piece. »This is the good kids' HQ. Max here.« He was glad not to be interrupted.
It was Kathrin, saying, »We've found the shop with the glass case! It's the zoo shop in Baker Street!«
»What, another glass case?« said Max in surprise. He turned to Thomas. »Listen, Kathrin has found the glass case, too, in the shop at the zoo.«
Thomas felt that this **boded no good**. He took the

that bodes no good: das bedeutet nichts Gutes, das lässt Böses ahnen

phone and said, »Stay where you are, and call back in half an hour's time. Then I'll tell you what else is going on.« He put the phone back on the stand and noted the latest call. And the phone was already ringing again. This time Thomas picked it up himself, although things were already moving too fast for his liking.

»Don't say you've found it, too,« he replied.

»What do you mean?« asked Christopher at the other end of the line. »We've found the glass case. So what kind of a reply is that?«

Thomas told him his group was the third so far to have found the glass case, and he wrote down the place: *Locksmith's shop in the High Street.* Then he gave Christopher the same message as he had given Kathrin just now.

»I said all along Ben's plan wouldn't work,« complained Christopher, ringing off.

»Seems like there's a lot of glass cases in this town, right?« said Max. Thomas silently agreed. He saw complications ahead of them all.

The Magician

Ben sat down on the floor of the school office, exhausted. »Nothing!« he groaned. »We've been going round shops for six hours, and no sign of any glass case with a key in it.«

»The others did better,« said Max. »They found the glass case all right.«
Ben was on his feet again in an instant. »What? You mean someone's found the glass case and you didn't tell us?« he said indignantly.
Thomas made a dismissive gesture. »Take it easy, Ben,« he said. »So far five different groups have found five different glass cases. They're all convinced theirs is the right one. And four of the groups are still out looking.« Thomas picked up his book recording incidents of special importance and read out loud: »One glass case at the hairdresser's in Little Garden Street, one in the shop at the zoo, another at the locksmith's place, and the fourth was reported in an hour ago. That one's in the Museum. Then the last was found ten minutes ago in the **DIY centre**.«
Leaning against the wall, Ben slowly **slid back** down to the floor. »Oh no!« he **wailed**. »And I bet none of them is the one we want.«
»Why not?« asked Max.
»Because those shops are places where there were glass cases with keys in them all along. Let's go through them. I know that hairdresser's in Little Garden Street. They have a counter with a glass cover and the key of the shop is always inside it. As for the shop at the zoo, well, the place is full of glass cases. I mean, just think of the aquariums. There's all sorts of stuff in them as decorations: old flower vases, toy

DIY centre: Abk. für Do-it-yourself-centre = der Baumarkt
(to) slide back: rutschen
(to) wail: jammern

ships, so I bet an old key is likely ,too. I don't think that one's our glass case.«

»And it's not exactly sensational to find a key on display in a glass case in a locksmith's,« added Frank.

»Or at the Museum or a DIY centre,« said Ben. »If you ask me, we have to look for a glass case that wasn't there before and appeared by magic because of the computer game.«

»Magic?« asked Max with interest. »Can computers do magic?«

»No, not really,« Ben told him, »although right now I'm not so sure myself. Because all this time the computer game's been doing things it shouldn't really be able to do."

»I don't understand,« said Max. He started playing with the magnifying glass again. The head teacher's desk began to smoulder.

»Max, I told you before, don't set the place on fire!« Thomas reminded the little boy. »Where did you get that magnifying glass anyway?«

Max stopped literally playing with fire. »In the staff room,« he said. »It was lying there next to the glass box.«

Ben **pricked up his ears**. »What glass box?«

»The one in the staff-room, of course,« Max repeated. »There's kind of a funny big glass box in it.«

Ben **leaped up** and ran to the staff-room. »I don't believe it!« the others heard him call. »Come here, quick. But mind where you **tread**!«

(to) prick up one`s ears: die Ohren spitzen

(to) leap up: aufspringen

(to) tread: treten

Frank, Thomas and Max hurried to join Ben. Arm outstretched, he was pointing to a big glass case with a **gilded** frame. A **copper-coloured** key lay on a bed of red velvet inside it. The key was glittering in the sunlight.

»Our glass case – the one we've spent hours looking for!« cried Ben. »Max, sometimes you are a real idiot!«

»What do you mean?« asked Max. »I found it, didn't I?«

Frank crossed the school yard to the small hall to tell the other children. They all came running, crowding around the staff-room door.

»Careful! Don't come any closer!« Ben warned them. »By my calculations the trapdoor is two metres away from the glass case. I just don't know how big it is.«

»But you can't see anything. It's a perfectly smooth floor. I don't see any trapdoor at all,« Jennifer objected.

Ben agreed with her, but all the same – »It must be there,« he said. »Look at that glass case. It wasn't here before, was it? Anyone ever been in the staff-room?«

»Yes, I have,« said Christopher. »I had an hour's **detention** after school once, and my teacher didn't want to sit on his own in the classroom supervising me, so he hauled me off here to the staff-room. I sat over there.« Christopher pointed to a place only about a metre from the glass case. »Ben is right. There wasn't any glass case here then.«

gilded: vergoldet
copper-coloured: kupferfarben

detention: der Arrest, das Nachsitzen

»But why is it here?« asked Martin. »I thought it was supposed to be in a shop?«

»I don't know why,« Ben admitted. »It *is* in a shop in the computer game. But if it's here that makes it easier to get Kolya to come up to school and negotiate. I mean, it looks perfectly natural to invite him to our HQ to do the deal.«

The others agreed, although they didn't quite like the idea of asking Kolya into their headquarters. But after all, they'd decided at their meeting this morning to take any risk necessary to set Miriam free and get the water back on again.

So in line with their plan they phoned Kolya and asked him to come up to their HQ and negotiate. Kolya agreed at once.

There was great excitement in the school: would Kolya come prepared for a peaceful discussion – or might he try to take their headquarters by storm and break the whole place up? Could they be sure he wouldn't **catch on** to their secret plan? And would the plan work this time? Would Kolya bring Miriam with him, as he'd promised, or leave her back at the waterworks as a **hostage**?

All these questions were going through the children's minds, but they didn't have much time to worry about them. They had their hands full getting **security precautions** in place.

In the gym, the children cleared all the mats aside and stowed their sleeping bags and the rest of their

(to) catch on: kapieren, durchschauen

hostage: die Geisel

security precautions: die Sicherheitsvorkehrungen

things in the room where the **apparatus** was kept. They didn't want Kolya to know just where the kids were sleeping in school. You could never be sure what stupid idea might occur to him some night if he had too good an idea of how they'd arranged their HQ. They also cleared the small hall and the main hall, making it look as if nothing had ever happened here.

apparatus: die Geräte, die Ausrüstung

Thomas locked up the caretaker's apartment again, and finally all the children split up into small groups and disappeared into the classrooms and basement of the school. So far Kolya didn't know just how many kids there were on Ben's side, and they didn't want him to know either. But their hiding places were chosen so that the children could keep an eye on all the most important rooms – the gym, the main hall and the small hall. If the worst came to the worst, they had the walkie-talkie radios with them.

Thomas had taken over the control centre in the school office again, and he only had to reach out a hand to sound the sirens. One false move from any of Kolya's gang would be enough – Thomas would hear about it at once by walkie-talkie. Then he would activate the sirens, and a moment later a hundred and thirty children would be ready to defend their headquarters against Kolya. Thomas checked by radio that they were all at their posts. Everyone was ready, and they had everything in working order.

And not a moment too soon, because Martin, up on

the roof of the tallest of the school buildings with a walkie-talkie and a pair of binoculars, was already announcing, »Watch out! Kolya's on his way! Oh, thank goodness, he has Miriam there, too. I don't think many of them have stayed at the waterworks. I'd say there are about thirty or forty people with him. Most of them armed. Wow, I just hope this works out!« Thomas received the news and passed it on to those of the other groups that had a walkie-talkie radio.

Ben was pleased. Standing beside Thomas with Frank, Jennifer and Norbert, he had heard the announcement, too. The four of them had been chosen at the meeting to conduct »negotiations« with Kolya – or more accurately, to lure Kolya into the trap. Ben felt his pulse speeding up. *I just hope I was right and the trapdoor's really there! What if the plan doesn't work? Then Kolya will insist on being recognized as our boss, and we'll refuse, and then he'll start a real fight in here! Oh no – the plan just has to work!*

(to) tap: tippen, antippen

Frank **tapped** Ben on the shoulder, bringing him back to reality. »Come on,« he said. »Time to go to the staff-room and meet Kolya.«

Frank, Norbert and Jennifer stationed themselves cautiously at the sides of the staff-room. Ben made his way **gingerly** along the wall and ended up standing beside the glass case.

gingerly: vorsichtig

Kolya marched into the staff-room and stopped in the middle of it, about two metres from the glass case.

Ten of the boys in his gang lined up behind him in the doorway. They were holding Miriam in the middle of them. Thomas had told her about the plan already. The rest of Kolya's gang spread around the corridors of the administration building and in the school yard.

***By my reckoning** Kolya is right above the trapdoor now*, thought Ben. Frank, Jennifer and Norbert looked at each other. They too had worked out that Kolya must be standing on top of the trapdoor.

by my reckoning: nach meinen Berechnungen

But nothing happened.

What do I do now? thought Ben. *Talk!* he told himself. *I must get Kolya involved in a conversation. Then perhaps he'll walk about a bit and finally tread on that trapdoor. It has to be there!*

»Well?« began Kolya. »What is there to discuss? I'm your boss and that's it!«

»Er,« said Ben, **hesitantly**. »The question is, what does that really mean? I mean, what happens to us if you get to be boss?«

hesitantly: zögernd

Kolya lowered his head, paced two steps to the right and then paced back again.

Why doesn't any trapdoor open? Ben asked himself.

Finally Kolya said, »Making the school an HQ is a good idea. And you lot have given me so much trouble it would be really funny to rule you from here. So first I'll be taking over this places as my own headquarters.«

»No problem,« said Ben. »But what are you going to do here?«

»Well, rule the city!« said Kolya.

Jennifer rolled her eyes. *The stupid boy hasn't the faintest idea what he really wants*, she thought, *let alone what has to be done in this city. He just wants to be boss.* Out loud she said, »We got that message loud and clear already, Kolya.«

Kolya turned to Jennifer and took a step towards her. *Still nothing! Where is that wretched trapdoor?* Ben felt himself getting more and more nervous.

Jennifer went on. »So what does ruling the city mean to you?«

(to) stammer: stammeln

Kolya began **stammering** slightly. »Well, same as ruling things usually means! Deciding what happens and what's allowed. I make the laws. Anyone who doesn't **obey** them gets locked up. My **lads** will be my police force, and they'll see everyone obeys me.«

(to) obey: gehorchen
lad: der Kumpel

Kolya felt he had thought of something extremely important. That was how he saw the way adults ran things: they made laws and had a police force to lock people up. Sounded good to him!

Frank groaned out loud. »Maybe we ought to put the question another way,« he said. »Listen, Kolya, think of a game of football. It has rules – laws, you could call them. And there's a **referee** to make sure the players keep the rules, like your police . . .«

referee: der Schiedsrichter

»Yes, exactly, that's just what I mean!« Beaming, Kolya went over to Frank and then back to Ben. »The way Frank explained it. That's just right!«

The trapdoor isn't going to open of its own accord,

thought Ben. *Obviously it has to be activated by something. How did it go in the computer game?*
»I haven't finished yet,« Frank went on. Kolya looked at him **inquiringly**. »We'll stick with the example of the football game, okay? We'd just like to know what the rules are going to be. If you're playing football you can't play by the rules if there aren't any. And you haven't made the rules yet. We want to know what your laws will be like.«

inquiringly: fragend

Kolya looked rather desperately at Frank. »Rules?« he stammered. »Laws?«
Frank, Norbert and Jennifer folded their arms and waited for an answer.
»Yes, oh great chief,« said Miriam sarcastically. »Tell us your laws, oh great master, so we can remember to keep them!«
Furiously, Kolya turned to Miriam. »And you're the first who'll be locked up if you go on answering back like that!« he shouted at her.
»But you're holding me prisoner already!« replied Miriam. »And I don't even know why. So what else can you do to me?«
Kolya was baffled. What Miriam said was quite right: he had taken her prisoner and he didn't know why himself. »Okay,« he said at last, generously. »Let her free. I'll give her one more chance. Until we have our laws. But then you'd better watch out.«
»Of course,« said Miriam in a **meek** tone – much too meek. She went to join Jennifer, and winked at her.

meek: nachgiebig; hier: brav

»Maybe we ought all to work out the laws together and then pass them?« suggested Jennifer.

»No way,« said Kolya automatically. »I'm the boss!«

The magician, thought Ben. *It's the magician who opens the trapdoor in the computer game!* While Kolya was still thinking about his laws Ben went slowly, step by step, around the glass case, stationing himself on the exact place where the magician in the computer game stood.

»The first law,« said Kolya at last, »the first law is that I make all the laws! That's a law, too, isn't it, right?« He looked inquiringly around.

»Yes,« agreed Norbert. »That's a law. Although rather a **loony** law.«

loony: bekloppt, behämmert

»You shut up!« Kolya yelled at him. He was feeling more certain of himself again now that he'd thought of a real law to pass. »And the second law,« he went on, »is that all the shops in this city belong to me. No one can take anything from them without paying. It's all mine!«

»What a great law!« said Jennifer. »And where are we going to get the money to pay for the things?«

»Even if we had any, what would you do with all the money you earned? I mean, if everything belongs to you already?« added Frank.

Kolya felt he'd been tricked. Why couldn't he think of any clever laws? »Shut up, will you?« he shouted.

I must do it now, thought Ben.

Kolya was still shouting. »What's the idea of all this garbage? There's just the one law, and it says I make the laws. So you'd better get used to the idea. I'M THE BOSS. That'll do for you, okay?«

»Yes, that'll do,« said Ben.

Jennifer, Miriam, Frank and Norbert looked at him in surprise. They'd lured Kolya into their trap so well – why didn't Ben spring it?

»Like we said on the phone, yes, you're the boss,« Ben went on. »And we accept that. We only want to know about the laws we shall have to keep.«

Miriam and the other three stood there, astonished. Their **jaws** dropped. *What was the matter with Ben? The wretched trapdoor still wasn't opening, and Ben was suddenly agreeing to Kolya's conditions! What about the plan?*

jaw: der Kiefer, die Kinnlade

»But you must keep your own promise. We need water, and we need it now!« Ben demanded.

Kolya nodded, satisfied. He snapped his fingers, and one of his bodyguards left the staff-room.

»It'll only take five minutes,« said Kolya. »Right, I've let Miriam free, and the water is about to be turned on again. But then I'm boss of this city, so no clever tricks! That's what we agreed!«

Jennifer, Miriam, Frank and Norbert stared blankly at Ben when he nodded to Kolya.

Now, thought Ben. *It just has to work! Like in the computer game*. He raised his head, stretched his arms out, laid his hands, palms downwards, on the glass case, and closed his eyes. *I want the trapdoor to open now,* he thought. *I COMMAND THE TRAPDOOR TO OPEN NOW!*

whirr: das Surren

for the fraction of a second: für den Bruchteil einer Sekunde

floorboards: die Diele, der Fußboden

agitation: die Erregung, die Aufregung

(to) get the upper hand over sb/sth: die Oberhand bekommen über jdn/etw

Ben heard a loud **whirr** in the room. There was an equally ear-splitting whistle, repeated three times. He felt the floor vibrate, and **for the fraction of a second** there was a sound like a lift going down in a department store.

»He's gone!«

»He just fell into the **floorboards**!«

»What happened?«

»Look – look at that huge hole in the floor!«

Kolya's bodyguards were all shouting in **agitation**. Ben opened his eyes again. Kolya had disappeared without trace. Ben found that he was trembling all over, and breathing hard. He could feel his heart beating wildly.

»Stay where you are!« Frank told Kolya's bodyguards. »Or you'll go the same way!« Frank hadn't the faintest idea how it had happened, but he had quickly caught on, and knew they had to use this moment of surprise **to get the upper hand over** the rest of Kolya's gang.

»The water's on again,« said the bodyguard who was just coming back from the phone in the school office. »Hey – where's Kolya gone?«

»He – he – he disappeared into the floor!« stammered one of the gang. »Don't move. Or the same will happen to you!«

»What's going on? How do you mean, disappeared into the floor?« asked the other boy.

»I don't know how they did it,« said the gang member, »but take a look at the floor!« He pointed to the middle of the room. There was a big hole there, about two metres square.

Norbert went cautiously up to the opening and looked in. There was nothing to be seen; it was all dark. Norbert had the impression that it was very, very deep. »Kolya?« he called down the hole. The sound of his voice echoed back from the opening. »KOLYA!« shouted Norbert again, a good deal louder this time. An equally loud echo came back. Norbert put his hands over his ears.

»He's down in a huge great labyrinth,« said Ben, who was still standing behind the glass case. »But there are plenty of rooms with food and drink in them. He won't starve. He'll just have to spend a long time thinking how to find the way out.« Ben thought about it for a moment. Then he added, »Since Kolya's not fond of thinking, it will probably be a *very* long time. Frank, would you see about the rest of the gang before I let them all go?«

Frank saw Ben's cunning idea. He knew that Ben couldn't repeat the same trick with the other gang members just like that, but *they* didn't know it.

»Go on, then!« ordered Frank **sternly**. »Tell your people they're all to assemble in the school yard – and unarmed!«

sternly: streng, ernst

»And our own people will meet at once in the small hall,« Jennifer decided. »Except for ten children – ten of us had better go with Frank to be on the safe side.«

puzzle: das Rätsel, das Puzzle

They all left the staff-room. Except for Ben. He was standing alone behind the glass case now. He stared at the big black opening in the floorboards. *What happened?* he asked himself. It was a **puzzle**. He went over all the possible moves in the computer game once again in his mind. Finally he decided: *There's no other answer – I was the magician in the computer game myself!* The thought sent a cold shudder down his back. But that was how it had been. There had been no sign of any trapdoor until he stood in the magician's place and, in his mind, spoke the command uttered by the magician in the computer game. The trapdoor had reacted; it had obeyed his command!
Ben was the magician! *Was?* he wondered. *Or am I still? And if I am, then what? What powers do I have, and how useful or dangerous are they?*
He hurried past the big hole, out of the staff-room and ran out of doors. He urgently needed fresh air – and some peace and quiet.

Save the Animals!

(to) drag: ziehen, schleppen
hose-pipe: der Schlauch, der Wasserschlauch
parrot: der Papagei

»The tigers first!« Kathrin was trying to **drag** a large, thick roll of metal out of a shed. It was wrapped around a **hose-pipe**, but the hose in its metal cover was too heavy. »Give me a hand!« she called to Christopher and Martin, who were just filling the **parrots'** drinking bowls with two buckets of water.

The two boys put their buckets down and hurried over to Kathrin. The three of them slowly managed to unroll the hose in the direction of the tigers' enclosure. They stopped at the fence.
»That ought to do,« Kathrin decided. »I can point the hose at the tigers' drinking pool from here. Thanks very much.«
Christopher and Martin went back to the parrots, looking in at the llama **enclosure** on the way. Norbert and Hannes were there filling up the animals' drinking **troughs** from another hose-pipe. Christopher and Martin nodded to each other, pleased, because only yesterday Hannes had been a member of Kolya's gang.
After Kolya's disappearance, Frank and Norbert had assembled all the gang members in the school yard and told them the situation in the city: how the computer game had made the grown-ups disappear, and it was very likely that everything would be back to normal if they could reach Level Four of the game by playing it according to the rules, but no one knew when and how it would happen, and until then they had **to fend for themselves**. That meant going very carefully with food, and looking after the animals in the zoo was a priority. It also meant taking care of the smaller kids, and all the children planning what they did next together. Because their only chance of surviving for what might be a long time was to make full use of everyone's abilities.

enclosure: das Gehege

trough: der Trog

(to) fend for oneself: für sich selbst sorgen

Then Frank showed Kolya's gang members round the headquarters, and explained how they were providing all the children with food and drink. No one had to be alone – they were looking after all the children including anyone who was sick, Frank said.

After this long explanation, Norbert and Frank left Kolya's gang free to join them or go away. »You can do as you like,« Frank had finished, »only don't make any trouble for us. Or you'll go the same way as Kolya and Siggi.«

About half of Kolya's group still didn't believe that Siggi had really disappeared. They thought he'd simply run away. But they had seen Kolya fall into the dark pit with their own eyes, and it gave them a healthy respect for Ben and his friends. And now Kolya was gone. There was no one left to tell them what to do, so many of them joined Ben's group. Twelve boys and seven girls in all, Norbert counted. The rest preferred **to strike out** on their own. They didn't feel like feeding animals or looking after little kids – they'd rather **roam the streets**, drive cars and drink beer.

(to) strike out: losziehen

(to) roam the streets: durch die Staßen ziehen

»Let them,« Frank had said. »They'll find it's dead boring some time. Maybe they'll come and join us then.« And they had let the other boys and girls from Kolya's group go, just under thirty of them. They wouldn't be making any trouble for the time being.

At the same time as Frank and Norbert were talking to the members of Kolya's gang who had stayed,

Jennifer was in charge of the meeting of their own people in the small hall. The children had soon come to an agreement – now that they had water again, the first thing was to give the animals in the zoo fresh water to drink. They all met for breakfast half an hour earlier than usual next morning, and set off for the zoo together.

»Hey, that one looks hungry and sad,« said Hannes, pointing to a llama standing away from the others in their enclosure. Its head was nodding in a rather funny way. Norbert filled a bucket of water and got the hose in place. Hannes looked around, found a small **patch of grass** beside the path, and pulled up a few **tufts**. Norbert and Hannes moved away from the other llamas, who were crowding round their trough enjoying the fresh water, and tried to **entice** the solitary llama their way. They succeeded: the sad-looking llama trotted slowly over to the two boys. It stopped just in front of them, and looked at them doubtfully with its head slightly on one side. Hannes held the tufts of grass out to the animal over the fence and talked soothingly to it. Norbert carefully lifted the bucket of water over the fence and put it down right at the llama's feet.

The llama hesitantly ate several of the tufts of grass out of Hannes's hand, chewing with obvious satisfaction. Then it bent its head and drank a couple of large **gulps** of water from the bucket. »It's working!« said Hannes happily. »It just didn't like to be with the

patch of grass: der Grasflecken
tuft: das Büschel

(to) entice: locken, anlocken

gulp: der Schluck

others. Maybe it's sick, so the others are avoiding it?«

»Or maybe it's the black sheep of the family so it always gets to eat last!« said Norbert for a joke.

»No, it's a llama,« replied Hannes seriously. Norbert was just about to explain that he had been trying to be funny when the llama suddenly raised its head and spat right in Hannes's face.

»Yuk!« cried Hannes. »It went and spat at me, the disgusting pig!«

»No, it's a llama!« laughed Norbert. In fact he was laughing so much he couldn't control himself. He fell on the ground, **clutching** his stomach and **rolling about convulsively** on the dirty path.

(to) clutch: greifen
(to) roll about convulsively: sich wälzen

Hannes ran back to the hose, turned it on and directed the water straight at Norbert.

Norbert yelled and shouted and tried to get away from the jet of water, crawling on all fours over the sandy and increasingly **soggy** ground. But Hannes wasn't **relenting**.

soggy: matschig

(to) relent: ablassen von

»What's going on around here?« asked Peter, who was passing with a metal bucket of something in his hands.

»Norberticus Muddicus!« said Hannes, giggling. »Also known as the Common **Mudlark**! I'm just giving it a cold shower!«

mudlark: der Schlammkriecher

Peter didn't think this half as funny as Hannes did. After all, Norbert had been one of his friends in the voluntary fire-fighters, though Hannes didn't know that. Anyway, Peter thought he ought to stand by his fire-fighting friend, and he **jammed** the metal bucket over Hannes's head.

The hose, still **spurting** water, fell from his hand, took on independent life like a **twitching** snake because of the water pressure in it, and gave the llamas a shower through their fence. **Bleating** in surprise, the llamas **chased off** over their enclosure. Hannes staggered about on the sandy path unable to see where he was going, tried to shout but just made funny sounds inside the metal bucket, and finally managed to get the horrible thing off his head. »What's the idea!« he croaked, spitting the stuff from the bucket out on the path.

»Hannes Stincus,« said Peter. »Also known as the Common Stinker. We've just been **mucking out** the monkey cage. That's what was in there!«

Hannes ran off, shrieking. Peter and Norbert **laughed like a drain**. Hannes ran along the path, raced round the bench, sprinted on, crossed a flowerbed and then a small lawn, and finally landed with a leap like a fish in a small pond, intending to wash the monkey dirt off. Twenty flamingos scattered, squawking.

»Oh, wonderful!« Miriam snapped at him. »Those flamingos had only just decided they could trust me a bit. I'm supposed to be taking them to feed over there – and now you come along, you great idiot, jumping into the water right in the middle of the flock of flamingos. Can't you bathe somewhere else?«

(to) jam: überstülpen

(to) spurt: spritzen

twitching: züngelnd

(to) bleat: blöken, meckern

(to) chase off: davonjagen

(to) muck out: ausmisten

(to) laugh like a drain: sich kaputtlachen

disgusted: angeekelt

Hannes told her the reason for his peculiar behaviour. He still looked **disgusted** when he mentioned the monkey muck.
»And now you're in the middle of the pool where the hippo pees,« laughed Miriam.
Hannes jumped up in horror, raced away from the water and through the zoo, yelling.
No need to be particularly sorry for Hannes, thought Miriam, *seeing that the hippos really have an enclosure of their own right the other side of the zoo.* She grinned as she watched him go.
»Hey, look what I've found.« Thomas came down the path holding out a tattered leaflet.
»What is it?« asked Miriam. She had given up trying to run after the scattered flamingos.
»A plan of the zoo,« said Thomas proudly. »Just what we could do with. It was on a bench outside the keepers' hut over there. I expect one of the keepers was looking at it when he disappeared.«
Miriam couldn't see that there was anything so special about the plan. After all, everyone who came to see the zoo was given a map of its layout at the cash desk, and she said so to Thomas.
»Yes, but this isn't just an ordinary plan for visitors,« explained Thomas. »This one is for the people who work at the zoo. It's much more detailed. For instance, it shows you here where all the storerooms for the animals' feed are. Most of them are down in that big cellar.«

That did interest Miriam. »So now it looks as if we can find enough for most of them to eat as well as giving them water!«

Thomas nodded, pleased. They both immediately ran off to look at the stores and the stocks of food there – or rather, Miriam ran, while Thomas came **panting** after her.

(to) pant: keuchen

»Slow down, can't you?« he called after Miriam. »Five minutes isn't going to make any difference! Or do you think someone else will get in first and eat the animal feed?«

How anyone could move so slowly was more than Miriam could understand – especially when they'd just made an exciting discovery. »If I waited for you we wouldn't be feeding the animals until tonight at the earliest,« she called back, and ran on to the cellar entrance.

But when she tried the door it was locked. Miriam turned to run back to Thomas. The key to the lock must be in the keepers' hut where he had found the plan.

On the way back, and from quite a distance, she saw Thomas strolling towards her at his leisure. When he saw Miriam he put his hand in his trouser pocket and brought out something shiny. He held it up in the air. »Is the door locked?« he called. »I thought so. I brought my skeleton key just in case.«

Miriam smiled and sat down beside the path. It would take some time for Thomas to reach her. *He's*

terribly slow, but you can rely on him when he does arrive, she thought.
At last Thomas had caught up with her. They went over to the cellar door, and Thomas **fiddled about** in the lock with his skeleton key. Miriam was surprised: though he was usually so slow, Thomas had the door open in a few seconds, just the way he had opened the door of the caretaker's apartment.

(to) fiddle about: herumfummeln, -fuchteln

»How do you do it?« Miriam asked **appreciatively**.
»If you're patient and not always **dashing about** the place you can get a whole lot done,« said Thomas, pushing the cellar door open. Then he and Miriam shrank back, disgusted.

appreciatively: anerkennend
(to) dash about: herumhetzen

»Heavens, what a stink!« cried Miriam, holding her nose. »Whatever do they eat?«
»Not chocolate bars, that's for sure,« Thomas teased her.
»They've got no taste,« **retorted** Miriam at once. »I can smell that!«

(to) retort: erwidern, zurückgeben

They stood in the entrance for a moment to get used to the stink. Thomas looked for a light switch, found it and put the light on.
He and Miriam were gazing at a huge storeroom stuffed with everything the animals could want to eat. Or so at least they both suspected, because they hadn't the faintest idea what some of the things spread out before them were: they saw seeds and dried fruit, flour of some kind, sacks of something that looked like grain, dried fish – or that was what it

smelled like – and some funny sort of powder, as well as crates of fresh fruit that didn't seem to be going bad yet. The potatoes were all right too, and there were obviously special feed mixtures of some kind as well.

»Tell you what, we'd better ask Kathrin,« said Miriam. »If any of us knows which animal eats what and how much of it, then she does.«

»And suppose she doesn't?« asked Thomas uncertainly.

»What would you do if I gave you a big chocolate bar with a large dollop of tomato ketchup on it for breakfast tomorrow?« asked Miriam.

Thomas made a face. »Yuk! Throw it in the bin!«

»I expect that's just what the animals would want to do if we give them the wrong food,« said Miriam. »We just have to find out what they like and what they don't.«

And that was what they did. Miriam and Thomas rounded all the children up, and between them they cleared a good many of the stocks of feed. Using **wheelbarrows**, they took the seeds and flour, grain and vegetables to the separate enclosures, guessing what they thought the animals' diet was. After seven hours of hard work they went back to school. Luckily they had left a small group of ten kids at HQ to make supper. In no time at all the children ate three large pans of mashed potato and over five hundred fish fingers.

wheelbarrow: die Schubkarre

Half an hour later, everyone in the gym had fallen fast asleep.
Except for Ben.

The Mystery of the Key

(to) spread: schmieren, bestreichen mit

»Where's Ben?« asked Jennifer at breakfast, **spreading** her second slice of bread and jam. »He didn't want to go to the zoo, I didn't see him yesterday evening, and he wasn't in his sleeping-bag this morning either. I'm getting a bit worried."
»I saw him just for a moment this morning,« said Frank. »I woke up when he was getting dressed. It was still very early. Ben said something about going to the staff-room.«
»The staff-room? This early?« said Miriam in surprise. »Sometimes I can't make Ben out at all. Why don't we go and see what he's doing there?«
The others agreed at once. Miriam put another couple of chocolate bars in her trouser pockets and then went off to the staff-room with Jennifer, Frank and Thomas.
Ben was in there, sitting in front of the glass case and staring at the key.
»Ben!« cried Jennifer. »What are you doing here?«
Ben turned slowly and signalled to his friends to sit down with him. At a loss, they did as he wanted.
»I can work magic,« said Ben quietly.

»You can do what?« Miriam jumped up.

Ben made the same gesture, indicating that he wanted Miriam to sit down again. He waited until she was sitting quietly once more and then went on.

»I've been sitting here since yesterday afternoon, thinking about what happened to me. You remember how the trapdoor suddenly opened up? It opened because I told it to.«

»You told the door to open?« Jennifer sounded **incredulous**.

incredulous: ungläubig, skeptisch, zweifelnd

Ben stood up, walked round the glass case, placed his hands on the glass cover just as he had when he was doing the deal with Kolya yesterday, and said, »Now, watch this!«

He raised his head, closed his eyes, and said: *»I COMMAND THE TRAPDOOR TO CLOSE!«*

The children heard that loud whirr in the room again. Then came the ear-splitting whistle, three times, just the same as before. The floor vibrated, and the trapdoor closed with the same strange sound of a lift going down.

Jennifer, Miriam, Frank and Thomas **gaped** at the floor. All they could see was a smooth surface. Nothing showed that there had been a big hole in the floorboards a minute earlier. Before anyone could utter a sound, Ben did the same thing the other way around.

(to) gape: anstarren

»I COMMAND THE TRAPDOOR TO OPEN!« he called. A few seconds later the hole was back.

»That's how the trapdoor opened yesterday?« asked Frank, astonished. »I did wonder why it took so long at first, and then the opening was suddenly there after all.«

»Yes, that's how,« Ben confirmed. »I remembered how it works in the computer game; the magician opens the trapdoor, and then in the end you have to **conquer** the magician by taking his place. And as the magician wasn't there at all yesterday, of course I could easily replace him. But that's not all. Watch this.«

(to) conquer: besiegen

Once again Ben straightened his neck and closed his eyes, putting his hands on the glass case in the now familiar way.

»I COMMAND DARKNESS!« he called, and next moment the five children were in a room as black as night.

»Don't do that, Ben,« begged Jennifer. »Put the light on again.«

»The light?« said Ben, somewhere in the darkness. »The light wasn't on. The sun was shining in through the window a moment ago. Now it's dark as night in this room. By magic.«

Then Jennifer heard Ben say: *»I COMMAND LIGHT!«*

And next moment the staff-room was as light as before.

»This is weird,« said Miriam. »What else can you do?«

»I've tried out all the tricks I know from the magician in the computer game,« replied Ben. »Trapdoor, darkness, mist, **sloping walls**, I even called up a **whirlwind** in this room yesterday afternoon. It all works.«

»Hey, that's great!« said Thomas happily. »We have a magician among us. That makes life much easier. If only we'd known before we could have spared ourselves all that trouble at the zoo. You could just have fed the animals by magic!«

»No,« Ben explained. »That's the **snag**: all I can do with this magic is destroy things and lure people into traps. Just like in the computer game. Only I've never got as far as the key in the game before because the magician has always stopped me.«

»Or the department store salesman,« said Frank, who had often been **turfed out** of the store with Ben in mid-battle with the magician. Indeed, that was why they'd never got beyond him.

»The worst thing,« said Ben, »is that I can do it by mistake, too. I'll show you.«

He went over to the large conference table in the staff-room, pulled out a chair, kicked it once, hard, and shouted, »*GO TO HELL, YOU STUPID CHAIR!*« Suddenly, out of the blue, the chair caught fire, flew across the room and disappeared in mid-flight. Jennifer and Miriam instinctively jumped aside. Frank had thrown himself flat on the floor; only Thomas was too slow. He just managed to duck his head. »The – the chair went to hell!« he stammered. »That's what I did with a chair yesterday. I'd bumped

sloping wall: die schiefe Wand
whirlwind: der Wirbelsturm

snag: der Haken

(to) turf out: hinauswerfen

into it, and I felt so cross I kicked it and then said that about hell. Just imagine if I did it with one of you by accident. Luckily I was alone in here yesterday,« explained Ben. »I have to get rid of this dreadful magic power again, understand? But I don't know how.«

They were all silent. Ben's demonstration of his magic power had been only too impressive.

In the silence, Jennifer could be heard swallowing hard. »This is awful!« she stammered. The others, **grave-faced**, silently agreed with her. What further surprises might the game have in store for them? Miriam felt her face flushing red with emotion. Frank **surreptitiously** wiped the **perspiring** palms of his hands on his trousers. He cleared his throat. »We've made it so far – I'm sure we'll manage somehow,« he said, hoping to cheer the others.

grave-faced: mit ernstem Gesicht

surreptitiously: heimlich
(to) perspire: schwitzen

»How?« asked Ben, trying hard not to let his voice shake too much with the fear he felt. Jennifer noticed, all the same.

We have to find a solution together, she thought, and said out loud: »What about that key in the glass case? Perhaps it has something to do with it? What part does it play in the game?«

»I don't know,« replied Ben. »Like we said, Frank and I never got that far in the computer game. But the key ought really to take you up to the next level, whatever that may look like. And I still can't get at it. I tried hitting the glass with a hammer, but there's just no way to open the case. I don't know what to do. I wish I

could get rid of this horrible magic power!« Ben's voice was trembling very obviously now.
The children said nothing. Ben really was in a terrible situation. Jennifer moved over to him and put her arm around him.
»I think Frank's right,« she tried to comfort him. »So far we've always found a solution, working together.«
But this time nothing seemed to **occur** to them. They were getting more and more involved in the rules of the computer game which none of them knew except for Ben and Frank – and even Ben and Frank knew it only up to the place they had now reached.
»Maybe,« Miriam began after a long pause, »maybe you just have to say clearly that you don't want to have the magic power.« She had really said that without thinking very much, but as she spoke she decided it wasn't such a bad idea. »I mean, that's what I do at the church disco, for instance.«
Ben looked up briefly and gave Miriam a **scornful** glance. *Church disco!* What did that have to do with his problem? Miriam was not **deterred**. She went on to explain. »When some **grotty nerd** comes and asks me to dance, I just say firmly *No*. And then the grotty nerd usually goes away.«
Ben couldn't hide his annoyance any longer. »Oh, don't be so silly!« he snapped at Miriam. »Here we are facing a serious problem – and you carry on about your stupid church disco.«

(to) occur: einfallen, in den Sinn kommen

scornful: verächtlich, spöttisch

(to) be deterred: sich abschrecken, einschüchtern lassen
grotty: mies, dreckig, ätzend
nerd: Depp

snottily: hochnäsig

Miriam herself wasn't entirely convinced that hers was a good idea, but when Ben reacted so **snottily** she felt she had to defend it on principle. »Well, maybe famous Brainbox Ben always does know better than everyone else,« she snapped back. »But I bet famous Brainbox Ben hasn't tried it yet.«

Frank, Thomas and Jennifer looked expectantly at Ben, who glanced quickly from one to another of them.

»Why are you staring like that?« he asked, sounding hurt. »Of course I haven't tried it. It's just too nutty – saying *no* like at the church disco!« Ben tapped his forehead with one finger.

»Oh, of course!« Miriam exploded. »Famous Brainbox Ben doesn't need to try anything out. Famous Brainbox Ben knows everything ahead of time. So never mind anything, you dwarf magician!«

His face flushed with rage and desperation, Ben jumped up from where he was sitting and shouted back: »You silly cow, I wish you were . . .« But at that moment Frank jumped on him, threw him to the floor and placed his hands over Ben's mouth. He had put so much energy into his jump that both boys rolled over and over on the staff-room floor, straight towards the big hole in the floor.

Miriam screamed and covered her face with her hands, Thomas was so horrified that he very nearly reacted as quickly as anyone else, and Jennifer dived at the two boys, who **were** all **tangled up** together, to

(to) be tangled up: verknäult sein

keep them from falling into the depths of the labyrinth. She clung to Ben's pullover, just managed **to hook** her right foot around one leg of the glass case, and that way she prevented Ben from rolling any further over the floor. Ben came to a sudden halt, whereupon Frank turned a **somersault** over him and slid into the black hole. With the kind of lightning reaction he had practised hundreds of times in karate training, his left hand shot out and grabbed the edge of the hole, **clinging** to the floorboards.

»Help him!« Jennifer shouted to Miriam. Miriam leapt to the edge of the hole and seized Frank's wrist. At the same time she put her other hand out to Thomas.

»Pull – get a move on for once in your life and pull!« she hissed at Thomas, and in his shock he did indeed react at once, hauling on Miriam's arm as hard as he could. Frank slowly worked his way up out of the hole, and ended up lying flat on the floor.

»Just in time,« breathed Frank.

»What on earth came over you all of a sudden?« asked Ben, gradually freeing himself from Jennifer's clutch.

»Didn't you realize?« Frank asked back. »You were just about to do something to Miriam by magic!«

Miriam went very **pale**. In her angry quarrel with Ben she hadn't noticed that Frank had saved her at the last moment. She thanked Frank **fervently**, and he was quick to respond. »You paid me back by pulling me out of the hole, Miriam. We're all looking after

(to) hook: einhaken

somersault: Purzelbaum, Salto

(to) cling: klammern

pale: blass, fahl

fervently: überschwänglich

(to) wean sb off sth: jdm etw abgewöhnen

everyone else here. About time we **weaned** Ben **off** the magic.«

»That's certainly right,« agreed Jennifer. »Ben, why not just give Miriam's idea a try?«

Ben had come around to it by now. He stood up, went over to the glass case, placed himself in his usual position and said: »Look here, thanks all the same, but I don't want to be able to work magic.« Then he tested it: he asked for darkness and it turned dark. He asked for light and it turned light again.

»I told you so,« wailed Ben. »I can still work magic.«

reproachfully: vorwurfsvoll

»Was that all?« asked Miriam, looking **reproachfully** at Ben. »I mean, is *that* what you call saying no?« She straightened her shoulders, put her head forward and let her tongue loll out of her mouth. Like a silly little monster she **waddled around** the staff-room, muttering quietly to herself, »I don't want to be able to work magic. No, I don't want to be able to work magic.« After this imitation of Ben, she stationed herself in front of him again.

(to) waddle around: umherwackeln

»Is *THAT* what you call saying *NO?*«

Ben went red and said, sounding hurt, »I can make myself look silly without your help, Miriam, thanks very much. So how do you suggest I say *NO*?«

Miriam went round the glass case, pushed Ben aside and stood in the proper magic position. She took a couple of deep breaths, raised herself on tiptoe and shouted at the top of her voice: »*LISTEN, MAGICIAN! I*

DON'T WANT TO WORK MAGIC! NO! NO! NO! I'M GIVING UP THIS WHOLE DRATTED MAGIC BUSINESS! GET AWAY FROM ME! RIGHT AWAY! WE CAN DO WITHOUT YOU! ***SHOVE OFF****, MAGICIAN!«*

Shove off!: Schieb ab! Hau ab!

Miriam had been shouting so loud she was bright red in the face. Thomas and Frank were still holding their hands over their ears, Ben was just gaping at her, and Jennifer had a fit of the giggles. That was Miriam all over! Whenever they went to the church disco together, and a particularly nerdy boy tried making eyes at Miriam, she used to **bawl** the poor thing out just the way she'd shouted at the ghostly magician. After that even the most thick-skinned and **conceited** boys couldn't be seen for dust.

(to) bawl: brüllen, schreien

conceited: eingebildet

As a result hardly any boy in town dared make up to Miriam, so Miriam had turned the tables and could take the initiative with the boys she really liked. The others usually left her alone. That was one of the things Jennifer had always admired about her friend.

When Miriam had her breath back, or partly, she turned quietly to Ben and told him, »*THAT'S* the way to say *NO*, Ben. You really ought to go to the disco more often.«

Ben cautiously made his way to the magician's place. He still couldn't imagine saying *NO* the same way as Miriam. But if he couldn't get rid of the magic by any other means he'd just have to try. Ben felt dreadfully silly, but he summoned up all his **determination** and shouted as loud as he thought he *could* shout (which

determination: die Entschlossenheit

was about half as loud as Miriam): »Magic, magician! Go away! I don't want to work magic any more, *I COMMAND YOU TO DISAPPEAR AND LEAVE ME ALONE!«*
Uncertainly, Ben looked around the little company. Miriam was the first to applaud enthusiastically. »Great!« she said. »You did that really well!«
Ben smiled awkwardly.
»Now, try it out,« said Jennifer.
Ben got into the magician's position again and said, »*I COMMAND DARKNESS!*«
It stayed light! Ben tried again. The moment he had given his order, the children heard a sharp sound. The glass of the case cracked and felt to the floor in pieces, **tinkling**. Ben jumped back.

(to) tinkle: klingeln, bimmeln

»What was that?« asked Frank. »Another kind of magic?«
»The key!« cried Ben. »We can get at the key! I gave up the magic power. Obviously you have to do it on purpose. *That's* the way to get at the key!« He struck himself on the forehead. »I'd never have found that out in the computer game!«
»What does the key unlock?« Thomas had carefully approached the pile of broken glass where the key lay.
Although he had a very large collection of keys, he'd never seen one like this before. It **glinted** with a coppery **gleam** in the sunlight; it was about the size of an ordinary door key, but it was **octagonal**, with three **wards** and five **unnotched** sides. Those five

(to) glint: glitzern

gleam: der Glanz

octagonal: achtkantig

ward: der Bart (am Schlüssel)

sides were an odd wavy shape. But the strangest thing about the key was that even its grip was shaped like a key, too. It was obviously a kind of double-headed key that could be used at both ends.

unnotched: frei

»There can't be a lock that will fit in the whole world,« said Thomas.

»I can't imagine where it would fit either,« said Ben. »But it ought to take us to the next level somehow or other.«

The children looked around the staff-room for a lock into which the key might go. It certainly didn't fit the door, which had a perfectly normal key in its lock. The cupboards were no use either.

»Perhaps we ought to compare it with all the keys in the whole school?« suggested Jennifer. »It may look different from any key we ever saw before, but perhaps one side of it is like some other key here?«

The others thought hers was a good idea, and Thomas went off to the school office to fetch his big key-ring, the one with all the school keys hanging on it.

The others waited in the staff-room, but Thomas didn't come back.

»Hey, come here!« he called from the office instead. »Here – I'm here in the headmaster's office!«

When the others arrived, they found Thomas standing behind the Head's desk, pointing at its large brown surface.

»There's a hole there!« Thomas said in surprise.

(to) char: anbrennen, verkohlen

(to) reveal: offen legen

brass: das Messing

»That'll be where Max **charred** it,« said Ben, going towards the desk.

»No, it isn't,« Thomas contradicted him. »It looks quite different. It looks like . . .«. He paused for a moment as if to make sure he had seen it properly. »It looks like a keyhole,« he said at last. »But a very peculiar one!«

Ben stationed himself beside Thomas and tried to put the key in the keyhole. It didn't fit.

»Turn it round,« suggested Thomas. »I'm sure the handle is a key, too.«

Ben turned the key round and put it in the lock handle first. It fitted! The children held their breath. Ben slowly turned the key to the right. It stuck. Then he tried it to the left. As he turned the key, one of the Head's large filing cabinets moved aside with a squealing sound.

»A secret door!« breathed Frank. The astonished children saw the large cabinet move away to **reveal** a thick, heavy wooden door. They cautiously went over to it. Frank tried the heavy **brass** door handle.

»It's open!« he called. He slowly opened the door and went through it. The others followed.

They were standing in a large, dark office. There seemed to be a big window on one side of the room, but it was covered with a dark blue velvet curtain. At the end of the room, under a huge picture with far too much black and dark brown in it, stood a desk at least twice the size of the headmaster's. To left and right of this desk stood two flags. The wall opposite the window consisted of a huge cupboard full of doors and drawers. About four metres from the desk, in the middle of the room, the children saw a low, round glass table with four big leather armchairs grouped around it.

»Do you know where we are?« asked Jennifer.

The others shook their heads.

»I do!« Jennifer answered her own question. »This is the mayor's office.«

»The mayor?« said Miriam. »But surely the mayor's office is in the town hall. And that's at least five kilometres away!«

Jennifer nodded. »All the same,« she said. »I once went on a guided tour of the town hall with my parents. And we saw this room. I remember it perfectly because I thought that huge picture on the wall was so **hideously** ugly. This is the **mayor**'s office!«

»Well, anyway, we've reached Level Three!« said Ben. »And we have no idea what's going to happen next!«

hideously: grauenhaft
mayor: der Bürgermeister

The Decision

»Take a look at that!« said Jennifer.

The children had no idea what they were supposed to be doing in the mayor's office, but Ben had insisted that they were now on Level Three of the computer game, so if the rules of the game had brought them here, there must be some point in it.

In the end they could think of nothing to do but make a **thorough** search of the mayor's office. Perhaps that might come up with something to indicate why the game had brought them here in such a strange way. After all, they were now five kilometres from school, even though they'd only walked through a doorway.

thorough: gründlich

Jennifer had opened one of the doors of the big cupboard and found a large metal crate on wheels. It had *To Be Shredded* written on it in large red letters. Feeling curious, Jennifer had opened the crate and rummaged around among the piles of papers lying inside it.

Now she had fished out a thick file and was excitedly calling the others over to her. »This really is the end!« cried Jennifer indignantly.

»What's up?« asked Thomas, who was still over by the desk, wondering whether or not to take the blue glass **paperweight** to add to his collection. As for Frank, he had made himself comfortable in one of the soft leather armchairs and didn't feel like getting up again at once.

paperweight: der Briefbeschwerer

»These are plans for a five-storey car park,« Jennifer explained. »And guess where it's going to be built?« No one could. There were already two multi-storeys in the shopping centre, and large car parks close to the smaller shopping streets, too.

Jennifer **ostentatiously leafed through** the sheets of paper in the file and told them. »Right next to our school. On the sports field!«

Frank shot up from the leather armchair like a jack-in-the box, »The sports field?« he yelped. »Are they crazy? So where's the sports field going, then?« He made for Jennifer and snatched the file from her hands.

»There's a drawing at the very end,« said Jennifer. Kneeling on the floor, Frank took several architectural drawings out of the **pile** and spread them side by side on the floor in front of him. The others got down beside Frank. Even Thomas slowly joined them, but still keeping one eye on that paperweight. It would go really well in his collection of glass.

»You can see it quite clearly here,« said Jennifer, showing them. »Our sports field is right where they've drawn in the car park. And there's no sign of a new sports field anywhere.«

It took Frank's breath away. »So where are we going to play games and hold athletics events?« he stammered. »They must be out of their minds!«

»You found it in the crate saying *To Be Shredded*,« Ben said to Jennifer. »Perhaps they've given up the whole idea.«

»But it says *First Draft* on the file itself,« replied Jennifer. »There could be a second draft by now, and that's why they threw the old one out. Come on, let's see if we can find anything somewhere else!«

ostentatiously: auffällig, demonstrativ
(to) leaf through sth: etw durchblättern

pile: der Stapel

stride: der Schritt

»There's a black folder on the desk, the kind my Dad has in his office. It has the stuff he's supposed to sign in it.« Thomas rose and went to the desk, but Miriam was well ahead of him. With two **strides** she was past Thomas, snatched up the folder and leafed through it.

»Here!« she cried suddenly. »Here's another draft. It says so.« And she read aloud: »*Second Draft, Multi-Storey Car Park Project. For Decision.*« Miriam quickly looked at the last page. »Oh, thank goodness, it hasn't been signed yet!« she said with relief.

»Why thank goodness?« asked Jennifer. »The mayor's not around anyway – any more than the other grown-ups are.«

»But they could be back some time,« said Miriam. »Only I tell you what – these plans won't be around then!« And with a determined expression on her face, Miriam rolled the file up and put it in the back pocket of her jeans.

Frank grinned at Miriam. »Good idea, Miriam,« he said appreciatively. »I just hope it works.«

»Well, this means I'm going to take that paperweight,« Thomas decided. He wasn't interested in sport, but he still thought it was mean and unjust of the mayor to deprive the school of its sports field. So if the mayor was planning to take away the sports field, he'd take away the mayor's paperweight. *Your own fault! Serves you right!* thought Thomas, picking the paperweight up from the desk.

As he did so, the door of the small cupboard under the right-hand side of the desk sprang open. It gave Thomas such a shock that he stood there rooted to the spot. Something was shining brightly inside the cupboard. Thomas bent down for a closer look.

»Good heavens!« he cried.

»Oh no – what is it this time?« Miriam sounded stressed. All these surprises were getting to be too much for her. She went round the desk to look in the cupboard. But Thomas put the paperweight back on the desk so as to have his hands free for his new discovery. No sooner had he put the glass paperweight down than the cupboard door closed again with a loud click. Miriam shook it, but **in vain**. The door wouldn't open.

in vain: vergeblich, umsonst

»That's odd,« said Thomas in surprise. »I only put the paperweight down here, that's all.« And as he spoke he reached for his collector's piece and raised it a little way from the desk again. The door suddenly sprang open once more, hitting Miriam. She tumbled backwards, rolled some way across the room, scrambled to her feet and shook her head.

»A door on a **spring**?« she stammered. »What a stupid idea!« And then she looked at the little cupboard and saw something shining brightly inside. »But that's . . .«

spring: die Sprungfeder

»That's a golden computer!« interrupted Ben, who had hurried over to the desk with Frank and Jennifer.

»Made secure with a secret door-opening device,« added Thomas. »The door is activated by the paperweight!«

(to) squat: hocken

All five **squatted** down in a semi-circle in front of the shining gold rectangle, looking at it in awe.

»How about turning it on?« asked Ben uncertainly. His fingers were itching to try out this mysterious and obviously valuable computer, but he was a little scared, too. *How would it react, what programs were stored in it, and what would they do?*

»Well, now we've come this far I want to know what it is, too,« said Frank. Ben agreed. He cautiously came closer to the computer, slowly put his hand out to the POWER button, pressed it and **swiftly** withdrew his hand again. The screen began flickering without any sound at all. No humming, no beeping, no crackling – nothing. The computer made not a single sound, something Ben had never known in any computer before. The screen went on flickering, and then the words came up, in gold letters:

ADULT CITY

Jennifer and Miriam exchanged inquiring glances. Frank scratched his head, and Thomas, lost in thought, almost put the paperweight back down on the desk, but remembered not to at the last minute and kept it in his hands. Ben looked silently at the screen, his eyes narrowed. He **frowned**. He was thinking hard.

(to) frown: die Stirn runzeln

Another message appeared on the screen, this time in gold lettering:
Give The Password
Password? What on earth could the password be?
»Well, that's it, then,« said Frank, **downcast**. »How does it expect us to know the password? We'll never find out what it is!«
He was about to stand up and simply forget about the golden computer, but Ben tugged his trouser leg. »Wait!« said Ben. »We can at least try.«
The **challenge** of solving a puzzle presented by a computer was too tempting for Ben to **abandon** it just like that. He'd often enough sat at home for hours in front of his computer, trying to work out errors, difficult programs and odd functions. And he'd usually managed to solve the problem some time, too – until he came upon the error in the **Kid City** game. But he'd tried with that one, and even now he was keen to crack the mystery of the password.
»Let's think about it,« said Ben. »What might the password for **Adult City** be?«
Thomas and Frank shrugged. They hadn't the slightest idea. The password might be anything. How could they be expected to find it out?
»Maybe something typical of grown-ups?« suggested Jennifer out loud. »Something that occurs to us at once when we think of adults?«
»That's possible,« agreed Ben. »Like what, for instance?«

downcast: niedergeschlagen

challenge: die Herausforderung
(to) abandon: aufgeben

»Orders!« said Miriam, the first with an idea. »If you ask me what's typical of grown-ups is that they're always giving orders: *Sit down this minute! Don't do that! Don't eat so noisily! Get washed! Mind you're home by nine!* Now I come to think of it, whatever my parents say to me it's always orders. Same thing at school: *Write that essay by tomorrow! Pay attention! Stop talking at the back there! You must go out into the yard at break!* Orders, all of them!"

»She's right,« Jennifer agreed. »Grown-ups talk to us as if we were dogs or something. They don't ask any questions, they don't say would we mind doing something, they just issue commands!«

»And you feed commands into a computer, too,« added Frank. »I think ›Command‹ would be a good idea for a password.«

The others all thought so, too. Ben typed in COMMAND as a password and pressed ENTER.

The screen flickered for a moment, and then, in silver letters, showed the message:

Wrong password!

Enter the correct password!

You have two attempts left!

»A pity,« said Miriam. »I'd have thought that could easily be the password.«

»Well, this is the mayor's computer,« Ben reminded her. »Maybe the password has more to do with the mayor than adults in general. The mayor governs this city – how about ›Government‹?«

That wasn't a bad idea either, the others thought, so Ben typed in the word and pressed ENTER.
Once again the screen flickered and then a message appeared, this time in brown lettering:
Wrong password!
Enter the correct password!
You have one attempt left!
»Oh, darn, only one chance!« groaned Ben. The children racked their brains, muttering words they thought typical of grown-ups in general or the mayor in particular:
»Punishment . . . anger . . . tidiness,« said Miriam.
»Money . . . property . . . no time,« thought Thomas.
»Punctuality . . . sense . . . work,« offered Ben.
»Achievement . . . training . . . excellence,« suggested Frank.
»Oh, it's just too difficult to decide,« moaned Jennifer. She stopped, then repeated the last part of her sentence again. » . . . difficult to decide.« Thoughtfully, she went on murmuring. »Command . . . government . . . difficult to decide . . . the mayor has to make difficult decisions. Adults make decisions. . .« She waited a moment and then said, her eyes very bright, »Why not try ›Decision‹?«
Ben was enthusiastic. »That's it. Of course! It's all about the decision! Look, here we are very close to Level Four of the computer game, and on that level it all depends on the decision you make.«
»What decision?« asked Miriam.

»The decision that says if you win or lose,« said Ben.
»Of course,« agreed Frank. »The game is getting close to its end. And the result of a game is decided at the end whichever way it goes. Like in sports. I'm sure ›Decision‹ is right.«
Ben typed it in on the keyboard at once. The screen flickered, and the picture of a city appeared in gold lettering.
»It's the same as the picture in the **Kid City** game – except in gold this time!« cried Ben. »We've reached Level Four!«
The difference was that Ben had no joystick for moving a figure, as he did in his game, but that didn't seem to be too much of a problem, for there were no questions on the screen. It just showed an empty city with nothing moving.
»So now what?« asked Miriam, moving rather closer to Ben. »What does getting to Level Four mean? What do we have to do now?«
»I wish I knew!« **groaned** Ben. »I don't know anyone who's ever reached this level. We'll just have to try it out.« He hit a key **at random**.

(to) groan: grunzen

at random: zufällig

The picture of the golden city did not change, but more writing appeared at the bottom of the screen:
Your first decision. School, park or city?
Please select!
Ben read the words aloud. He hesitated.
»Try school,« said Jennifer. »We know that best, so we can do what the game wants us to do there.«

Ben selected. The broad outline of a school appeared on the screen, all in gold again. At the top left of the screen a black figure appeared:

10,000

And at the bottom a new question appeared:

Do you want to demolish the gym?

»What kind of stupid question is that?« said Frank indignantly. »No, we do not want to demolish the gym!« Ben firmly typed in NO. The black 10,000 disappeared. Instead, a red 100 appeared, winking on and off. The computer beeped! It was the first time it had made any sound at all. In the middle of the picture a red box appeared with white lettering inside it:

Warning!

Your first wrong decision.

You have only 100 points left.

Borderline area

The words **Warning** and **Borderline area** kept winking.

»Well, look at that!« said Frank, astonished. »How come it's a wrong decision not to demolish a gym? What kind of weird game is this?«

»Can you reverse the decision?« asked Jennifer.

Frank was about to turn indignantly on her, but she stopped him with a gesture. »I only want to find out what the game wants us to do,« she said. »Anyway, it *is* only a game.«

»Or let's hope so,« said Ben, hitting several keys that

he thought might reverse his last decision. It worked. Once again the question came up: did he want to demolish the gym? This time Ben said yes.

Your first correct decision.

Congratulations

said the computer happily, marking up 30,000 points.

Frank snorted indignantly, but the computer was already asking the next question:

Do you want to stay in school or move
to the park or the city?

it asked.

»Let's move to the city before it asks us to tear the whole school down!« said Frank.

Ben hit the key for the city.

»Ben! Frank!«

»Jennifer! Thomas!«

The five children turned. Who was calling their names? The calls were repeated.

»Surely that's Norbert's voice?« said Frank. »Where's it coming from?«

»The next room!« said Jennifer.

»The next room?« said the surprised Ben. »But Norbert ought still to be in the school, and that's five kilometres away! He can't know that we're in the town hall. We don't know how we came to be here ourselves.«

»All the same, that's Norbert's voice, and it's coming from the next room,« insisted Jennifer. She stood up, went to the door through which they had come, opened it and went into the next room to look for Norbert. After going two paces she stopped in astonishment. She was back in the headmaster's office five kilometres away from the town hall.

»Hi, Jennifer! Where've you been? And where are the others?« Norbert strode towards her.

Jennifer was still astounded. »The . . . the town hall . . . next door,« she stammered.

»Listen, Jennifer!« Norbert interrupted. »Where are Ben and the others? The gym has disappeared!«

»What?« Jennifer thought she couldn't have heard correctly.

Norbert repeated it. »The gym's gone! One moment it was there and the next it wasn't! It's simply gone! There's just a patch of sand left. Where are the others?«

Jennifer couldn't reply to him. She just called: »Miriam! Ben! Come here, quick! Frank! Thomas!«

The door opened and all four came running in.

»What's up?« cried Frank, and then stopped abruptly. So did the others. They turned round in surprise, finding themselves back in the Head's office. They'd simply walked through a door – travelling five kilometres in the process! Norbert gave them no time to **marvel at it**. He repeated that the gym had gone, and they all hurried outside to see this impossible thing. A gym didn't just disappear all of a sudden!

(to) marvel at sth: über etwas staunen

Only Ben turned suddenly and ran back through the door. Norbert, Jennifer, Miriam, Frank and Thomas were standing in the school yard looking in horror at the place where the gym had stood only a little while ago. The other hundred children were racing around, shouting at each other, **frantically** suggesting different ideas about what could have become of the gym. Norbert was about to explain how he had been there when it disappeared, when all of a sudden the gym was back. The big, old, ugly building stood there as if it had never been away. A hundred children flinched back, and the frantic argument about what could have happened began again. Norbert sat down in the middle of the school yard. This was too much for him. »So what was *that*?« he muttered quietly to himself.

frantically: erregt, aufgeregt

»Ben!« cried Jennifer. »That was Ben!« And she was running back to the Head's office. Miriam and Frank immediately followed. Thomas was about to turn and follow the others, too, but as she ran Jennifer called back to him to stay and explain to the rest of the kids what was going on. Thomas obeyed, and sat down beside Norbert.

Jennifer, Miriam and Frank **burst** through the door into the mayor's office. It worked again: once through that door they were in the town hall, five kilometres from school. The children stopped wondering about that. It was so, and that would have to do for the moment.

(to) burst: platzen

Ben was sitting at the golden computer, concentrating hard.
»Was that you with the gym?« asked Jennifer.
»It's back, right?«
Jennifer nodded **vigorously**.
»I thought so,« said Ben. »I'm back in the city now, and the computer's asking what I want to do with the trees.«
»What trees?« asked Jennifer. »There aren't any trees in the city.«
»A hundred and twenty-eight of them, according to the computer,« replied Ben. »And I bet if I say I want them **grubbed out** I'll have any number of points again, *and* the trees in the city will really disappear!«
»You think . . .?« Jennifer didn't like to say out loud what she was thinking. Ben understood, all the same, and finished her sentence for her. »Yes, obviously on Level Four everything I type in really happens. Level Four is **Adult City**!«
»Like in your **Kid City** computer game,« Miriam remembered. »That turned real, too, when all the grown-ups really did disappear from town.«
Ben nodded slightly, frowning and biting his nails.
»Two games?« said Frank in surprise. »One for kids and one for adults? I thought it was all the same game and now we'd reached Level Four? I don't understand.«
»Oh yes, you do, Frank,« said Ben at last. »It *is* the same game. And we're in the middle of it.«

vigorously: energisch, heftig, aufgeregt

(to) grub out: ausgraben, abholzen

»What do you mean, we're in the middle of it?«

»Until now we thought everything here was happening the way it does in the **Kid City** computer game, and the computer and its rules influenced the real world. And we thought that was why the grown-ups disappeared.«

»Are you saying that's not right?«

»Not entirely,« said Ben.

(to) spare: ersparen

»Then we could have **spared** ourselves all that trouble getting to Level Four?« Miriam feared the worst.

»No, far from it,« Ben said soothingly. »The real world doesn't work the same as the game. We're the game ourselves.«

»What?« said Jennifer. »I don't get it.«

Ben explained again. »It may sound crazy, but it's really perfectly simple. We're playing the game **Kid City**. Only not on the computer, we're right inside the game ourselves. It's not the grown-ups who've disappeared, we have! We're the live little figures on screen. So it's a case not of getting the grown-ups back but of getting us out of the game and back into real life. This is totally weird.«

(to) pinch: kneifen

Jennifer looked down at herself and **pinched** her own bottom. »I don't feel like a figure in a game,« she decided.

»I still don't really understand,« objected Miriam. »So what about the **Adult City** game?«

»It's Level Four of our game,« Ben explained. »We had to go through the whole computer game. First the grown-ups disappeared and we had to organize ourselves. That was Level One. Then I took over the magician's powers by replacing him. And that took us to Level Two. On Level Two it was up to us to **renounce** the magician's powers. That brought us the key that took us to Level Three in the mayor's office. And that's how we managed to make the jump from school to the town hall although it's five kilometres away.«

(to) renounce: verzichten

»How come?« asked Jennifer. »What does the distance have to do with the game?«

»Well, that's how I found out that we're in the game ourselves,« Ben went on. »In a computer game the levels jump from one event to the next. You simply see a new picture appear. And that's what happened to us. We've jumped from one picture to the next, from school to the town hall. That's what proved it to me: we *are* the game!«

»So go on. You were saying we'd reached Level Three,« Miriam pressed him.

»On Level Three we had to find the gold computer and boot it up. And then Level Four began, **Adult City**.«

Frank couldn't quite follow Ben's train of thought. »So what does this **Adult City** mean? How does the game go on now?« he asked.

»Well, when we've gone through all the stages of the game,« Ben repeated, »Level Four takes us to the world of grown-ups. We have to make the kind of decisions adults make. We were supposed to make the gym disappear, or the trees . . .«

»Just like the mayor's plan to build a car park on the sports field,« Frank interrupted him.
»It's true, only grown-ups would think of things like that!« said Jennifer.
Miriam nodded agreement. »I hope we're not going to go on playing it that way any more,« she said.

crucial: entscheidend

»Well, that's the **crucial** problem,« replied Ben.
»How do you mean?« asked Frank.

suspicion: der Verdacht

»Although we've only just found out that we're the game, our original **suspicion** was right, too, when we thought we could only get back to the old world with grown-ups in it by playing the game to the end.«

(to) nick (inf): klauen, mitgehen lassen

»Hold on a minute,« said Miriam. »You don't mean this seriously? After I just **nicked** that horrible plan so cleverly, do we really have to put it into practice ourselves?«
»Something like that,« agreed Ben. »We have to play the game to the end. Then, like any other computer game, it'll go back to the beginning. And the beginning is where we're in our old world with our parents and all the other grown-ups!«
»But to get there we have to make these stupid decisions, like tearing down the gym, grubbing out the trees and goodness knows what else!« said Jennifer indignantly.
Ben nodded. »That's exactly the kind of decision this golden computer wants us to take. Either we make typical adult decisions – against our will . . .«
». . . or we stay in this world with only kids and we

never see our parents again!« finished Jennifer, who now realized exactly what they were up against. She would almost rather she didn't.
The children fell silent. They faced an unavoidable decision in a cruel computer game. And Jennifer had the feeling that whichever way they decided, they would never be happy with that decision.

All's Not So Well that Ends Well

»I want to go back to my Mum and Dad!« Little Max hadn't followed many of the long explanations Ben gave at the meeting, but he did understand that he was never going to see his parents again if they switched off some funny old golden computer in the mayor's office. He had waited like a good boy for Ben to finish, he even listened patiently to what other kids had to say, but now he couldn't help it. Norbert had been **making a strong case** for never going back to their parents but staying in the world of children.
Max stood in the middle of the school hall crying. »I thought Mum and Dad had only gone away for a little while. Like on vacation. And then I thought it was quite fun being here with the rest of you, but now I want to go back to Mummy and Daddy!«
»I know just how you feel, Max,« said Miriam, trying to comfort the little boy. »But think of that horrible golden computer! It wants us to give up so many nice

(to) make a strong case: energisch/heftig für etw plädieren

things: the gym, the trees in the city, the sports field – next to go might be the little kids' playgrounds and all their toys. The idea of the game is to get rid of everything that's important to kids but no fun for adults. What are we going to do in the adult world without any of the things we like?«

»But what are we going to do here in this city full of kids without our little brothers and sisters and without our parents?« objected Kathrin. »I know I miss mine. And it can't work out in the long run. We're only living on food and stuff the grown-ups left behind.«

»We'll manage somehow,« said Norbert, trying to win her round. »We've managed everything so far.«

(to) support: unterstützen, Recht geben

But Christopher **supported** Kathrin. »And what happens on the day all the shops are empty, nothing left at all? Where are we going to get more food from, then?«

»We can grow it or rear it ourselves.« Torben spoke up. »I always go to see our cousins on their farm in the holidays. I've helped with everything: sowing, the harvest, milking cows, mucking out the stables, I was even there when they killed a pig. I know how it's done.«

»Me, too,« said Silvia. »I've been to stay in the country several times, too. I helped with work on the farm.«

»You don't seriously think we can do it all without the grown-ups?« interrupted Kathrin. The mere idea of having to kill an animal herself almost made her ill.

»We'll have to one day,« Thomas pointed out. »Grown-ups were kids themselves once. And we'll be grown up some time and have to do everything. The only difference is that on our own we have to learn how much faster.« Thomas sighed heavily as he put that thought into words. Doing anything fast was exactly what he didn't like.

»We're not getting anywhere,« groaned Jennifer. »We've been over every aspect of the problem at least three times in these last two hours.«

»So?« said Christopher. »What do you want to do now?«

Jennifer shrugged her shoulders. »I don't know,« she admitted. »But anyway I don't want to go back if it means everything we kids like is going to be taken away.«

»I agree,« said Ben, who thought it was about time this meeting made a decision.

»No gym and no sports field? Never!« Frank decided. »I'm staying in Kid City!«

Miriam hesitated to make her own decision. She thought she had never had such an interesting, exciting time before as she had had this week. They had been a real community, facing all their dangers and **solving** all their problems together. They'd fetched the sick kids from the hospital, built up stocks of food, put out a big fire, found accommodation for over a hundred children in their big HQ, made sure everyone had food and drink, they'd looked after the

(to) solve: lösen

little kids, protected and comforted them, they'd outwitted Kolya and his gang, they'd even looked after the animals in the zoo. Miriam had learned a lot this week, and she'd had a lot of fun, too. But did that mean she must never see her little brother and her parents again?

»I want it all to be the way it was before,« wailed Max, bringing Miriam back to **reality**.

reality: die Wirklichkeit

»Yes, that would be best,« Jennifer agreed. »But it seems that's not an option. The computer game we're in wants us either to be like adults or to stay in Kid City.«

Stay in Kid City? Jennifer's words echoed in Miriam's head. *And what about older boys?*

»It's horrible!« cried Kathrin. »Who'd think up such a mean game?«

»Obvious: it was grown-ups of some kind!« Jennifer told her.

Miriam returned to her own thoughts.

All the boys will disappear when they get to be fifteen. So will I have to go around with boys my own age or younger all the time? Miriam raised her head, but not to look at anything in particular; she was staring into space, **lost in thought**. *Hang on a moment, it's not just the boys who disappear when they're fifteen, we all will on our fifteenth birthdays! Like Siggi a few days ago.*

lost in thought: gedankenverloren

»We'll never grow up, though!« she shouted suddenly at the meeting. »Never mind how fast we learn, we'll only just have found out how to do something and then we'll disappear. We'll all disappear when we're fifteen. Just like Siggi! Kids can only stay in Kid City until their fifteenth birthday.«

Miriam was getting all worked up. The other children were much struck by her idea. They had forgotten all about that.

They wouldn't be able to be the community they were now for very long. The eldest of them would disappear, one by one. Even if it was two or three years before many of them went, in the end there would be a smaller and smaller group of children left, with no chance of surviving. Oh no! *They couldn't stay in Kid City!* But they didn't want to go back to the world of adults either – or not under these conditions!

»We're **trapped**,« said Jennifer at last.

(to) be trapped: in der Falle sitzen

»Yes,« groaned Miriam. »And most important of all, who knows where we go after we're fifteen? I don't think I want to know where Siggi is now.«

Ben's face suddenly broke into a beaming smile. »Miriam, sometimes I could kiss you!« he said.

»Go ahead!« cried Miriam promptly, with a sly sideways glance at Jennifer, who turned red.

Ben took it back at once. »I didn't mean **literally**! Anyway, now I know where we go when we get to be fifteen – back to the real world. To where the grown-ups are, which is where we want to go. Well, it's perfectly logical!«

literally: wörtlich

Jennifer pricked up her ears. »You mean we have to

stick it out here another couple of years and them we go back automatically?«

»That's one possibility,« agreed Ben. »But maybe there's another one, too.«

»What is it?« asked Jennifer, hopefully.

»Well.« Hesitantly, Ben began thinking of his answer. »It was a computer program got us into this trap. But computer programs are thought up by people.«

»So they can be altered by people, too!« said Frank in excitement, catching on to the way Ben was thinking.

»Yes, that's what I mean,« Ben agreed. »There are no computer programs that are just *there* and can never be altered.«

»So you think we can change the golden computer's program?« Miriam span round, looking for hopeful agreement in the other children's faces.

But no one was looking at her. All eyes were turned expectantly on Ben. Did he really think they could change the programming of the golden computer? And if so, how?

»We'd just have to make the computer think we're all fifteen already!«

»But we can't! I'm only nine!« objected Max, who hadn't been able to follow much of the conversation so far.

Ben grinned. »Ah, but the computer doesn't know that. It only knows what you feed into it.«

»So we tell the computer lies, see? Like we tell the

teachers lies when we're late for school.« Miriam sometimes drew odd comparisons, but at least Max now understood what it was all about.
»We have no other chance anyway,« said Ben, »so we might as well try it!«
A shout of delight echoed through the hall. No one knew if trying to trick the adults' golden computer would work, but at least the idea held out hope, and that was something. Talking and shouting excitedly, **faces flushed**, hands trembling, the children ran into the Head's office and then made for the door into the town hall.

faces flushed: mit roten Gesichtern (eigentlich: erröten)

»Wait – don't push like that! This won't do!« Ben was standing in the doorway between the two rooms that were really five kilometres apart. His nose was pressed against the door, and he was **bracing** his back against the crowd trying to get in. There were about twenty children in the mayor's office already. The others were trying to force their way through the door and find a place from which they could watch the golden computer.

(to) brace: stemmen

Frank came back from the mayor's office to help Ben. He pushed the throng of children back as hard as he could. »We won't all fit in!« he shouted. »Wait here!«
He was rewarded with a shout of **indignation**. Everyone wanted to be there watching to see if the golden computer could be tricked.

indignation: die Entrüstung, der Unwillen

Ben took a deep breath. He turned round, with difficulty because of the crush, and shouted: »Look, I'm sorry, but if you're all in the room we won't be able to do anything. If you want us to try you'll have to stay out here!«

(to) grouse: meckern, schimpfen
(to) grumble: murren

The children **groused** and **grumbled**, but they gave in. Sitting on the floor of the staff-room and the corridor outside it, they reluctantly settled down to wait.

Ben sat down at the golden computer and switched it on. Frank, Miriam and Jennifer were right behind him, with another twenty kids in a semi-circle further back.

The screen flickered in the usual way and brought up the words:

ADULT CITY

Then came the request for the password. Ben typed DECISION. The screen flickered again and then showed the picture of the city as it was in the **Kid City** game, except in gold.

Ben paused.

»Next will be the question of whether to choose the school, the park or the city, but by then we've probably already gone too far. I think this is where we ought to break into the program.«

»How?« asked Thomas behind him.

Ben didn't reply, but hit several keys.

The question about where they wanted to go appeared on screen.

»Oh no!« groaned Ben. »The game's going on. I can't get into the program here.« He pressed the RESET button. The game stopped and the computer restarted.

Once more the gold lettering came up:

ADULT CITY

Ben stopped the game at once. »I don't know how to get into this program,« he muttered. »The game always comes up at once.«

»That's just typical of adults,« muttered Miriam. »They won't let you see behind the scenes!«

»Yes,« agreed Frank. »In the **Kid City** game you can easily get into the program. A pity this one isn't constructed on the same principle.«

Ben looked at Frank, wide-eyed. »I wonder if that would work?« he asked.

»If what would work?« inquired Frank.

»What you just said,« replied Ben. »Take over the structure of **Kid City** and move it into this game?«

Frank still didn't get the idea.

Ben explained. »What do you think would happen if we tried to beat the game with its own weapons? I mean if we could copy **Kid City** into **Adult City** and **merge** them?«

(to) merge: miteinander verschmelzen, ineinander übergehen

»In the worst-case scenario it'd lead to chaos in both programs,« Frank suspected.

Ben had feared that too. He was frowning with anxiety. »All the same, we have to try.«

The other children agreed.

»Right, let's have a rest and I'll fetch my computer game from home,« Ben suggested, switching off the golden computer.

He was planning to get out into town through the

Head's office, but as soon as he stepped into the room the waiting children mobbed him.
»How's it going? Have we done it?
»Have you altered the program?«
»What's going on now?«
Questions rained down on Ben. He immediately turned and went back into the mayor's office.
»I'll never get through there,« said Ben. »Someone must go out and tell the others what the situation is.«
Jennifer offered, and went into the room next door with Ben. As she embarked on a long explanation, Ben hurried out into the school yard and mounted a racing bike that was standing around there.
He cycled home like the wind, went into his room, and snatched up the CD and several adaptors, cables and plugs that were lying about. Then he raced back to school at the same fast speed.
Although the others had used the time to take the gold computer carefully out of its cupboard in the desk and stand it on the floor, they felt as if Ben had been gone for days, although in fact he was back in just under half an hour. Out of breath, he stumbled into the mayor's office.
»There you are at last!« said the other children. Ben was too breathless to reply. Putting his hands in his trouser pockets, he brought out his assortment of plugs, cables and adaptors, and finally the CD of the **Kid City** game
»So now what?« asked Jennifer.

»Now I'm going to load the **Kid City** game,« explained Ben. Then I'll reprogram it. I'm going to tell the game there are no children in Kid City because everyone here is over fifteen.«

»And if there are no kids, then no one can be brought up to be an adult,« said Jennifer, getting the idea.

The children grinned at each other with **conspiratorial** expressions. Ben sat down in front of the computer beside Jennifer and put the CD-ROM into its compartment.

conspiratorial: verschwörerisch

»This is getting exciting,« said Frank. »**Kid City** loads itself when you put it in, but so does **Adult City**. I wonder what the computer's going to do now.«

Miriam bit her lower lip and **clasped her hands tight**. Frank was sitting cross-legged behind Ben, rocking back and forth.

(to) clasp one`s hands tight: die Hände zusammenpressen

Thomas was looking down at the paperweight. He had it on his lap, and he kept stroking it without noticing what he was doing.

Max moved close to Miriam and snuggled his head against her shoulder.

The screen flickered. A short beep. The usual lines in yellow came up and disappeared again. Then new wording:

Please wait. . .

»It's working!« whispered Ben in excitement. »It's loading the game!«

Quivering with excitement, the children moved closer together. Finally a high-pitched, simple tune

rang through the room, and then the screen announced:
KID CITY
Adventure Supergame from Computergames Inc.
At last the screen showed a city. That's how it all began, Ben remembered.
He quickly pressed several keys. No one saw which they were and how Ben did it, but suddenly there was nothing on screen but long, endless rows of figures. Ben moved confidently around in these rows of figures as if he'd been doing it all his life.
The children looked first at each other, then back at the screen. They hadn't the faintest idea what was going on.
Ben hit two more keys. The screen went as black as it was at the beginning. »There we are,« he said, taking a deep breath. »Done it!«
»Done it?« asked Jennifer blankly. »But there's nothing there!«
»The game's been reprogrammed. Now we just have to load the Adult City game and see what happens.«
Ben loaded it.
Nothing happened at all!
The screen didn't flicker, it just stayed black.
Silence.
The computer made not a single sound, and nor did the children.
There was a **deathly hush**.
»Oh, darn it!« **cursed** Ben. The sound of twenty chil-

deathly hush: die Totenstille
(to) curse: fluchen

dren sighing was like a great gust of wind blowing through the room.
Ben tried one last time. He restarted the computer. With the same result as before: nothing.
»It's no good,« said Ben, resigned. »It won't load any more the program we want to trick.« The children looked at each other, downcast. Their last chance, and it wasn't working.
»Now what do we do?« It was Miriam who broke the silence of the room with this question.
»We'd better tell the others,« Jennifer suggested. »And hold another meeting to decide what to do next.« She got up and went through the door into the staff-room.
A few seconds later she ran back into the mayor's office. »It's gone!« she cried. »The staff-room has gone!« The children jumped up and ran to the door.
»There's only an empty office next door!« Jennifer called after them. Frank reached the door first and flung it open. All the children stood there as if turned to stone. On the other side of the doorway they saw a small office, as plain and ordinary as any other small office in the world: a desk, two filing cabinets, a couple of phones, two chairs at the desk and three pot plants on the window-sill. That was all there was, where a few minutes ago there had still been the staff-room full of a hundred children crowded together, waiting impatiently to see what Ben would do with the computer.

»Where's the staff-room gone?« asked Miriam, cautiously putting her head through the open doorway.
»No trace of the others,« said Frank, who was standing in the little office looking round with astonishment.
»Have we gone through the wrong door?« asked Max.
»Can't have done,« replied Miriam. »There are only two doors here, this one leading to the staff-room and that one leading to the corridor in the town hall.« She pointed to a large, heavy oak door **adorned** with a lot of carving. Then Miriam gave a start of alarm, for just as she pointed the door out to Max, its handle moved slowly down. Miriam swallowed, hardly daring to move. The big, heavy door opened, but only a little way. Then it stopped again. A **cackle of laughter** could be heard outside. Now the other children realized what was going on too, and turned in alarm. What kind of voice was that? No kid ever laughed that way!

(to) adorn: schmücken, zieren

cackle of laughter: das gackernde Lachen

»Well then, Martha, see you downstairs,« croaked the voice, interrupting itself with a loud, hoarse cough. »Oh, my poor bronchitis!« it complained. The door moved again, opening a little further.
Holding their breath, the children stared at the door in suspense. They saw a hand come round it, a hand holding a bucket of water. They heard a foot pushing against the door, and then it opened fully. A woman stood there.

She was an old woman in a dark blue overall and a pale blue **headscarf**, with a small grey fringe of hair showing on her forehead. The woman stopped and looked at the twenty wide-eyed children staring at her.

»What are you kids doing here?« asked the woman. »The place closed hours ago! Where's your teacher?«

»Our what?« asked Miriam. Her voice shook.

»Your class teacher,« repeated the old woman, evidently surprised by this question. »If you're seeing round the town hall I suppose you have your teacher with you. Your teacher ought to know we close at seven.«

The children looked at the woman as if she had just landed in the room in the Spaceship Enterprise, and was still hand in hand with Mr Spock.

»What's the matter?« asked the woman. Her voice sounded a little more annoyed. »Lost your tongues, all of you? I want to know where your teacher is. I have to clean in here now, so you'd better clear off.«

»Er – our teacher disappeared!« replied Jennifer truthfully. »But where did *you* come from?«

That made the woman really cross. »Where did I come from? Such **impertinence**!« she grumbled. »I'll tell you where I come from: I've been cleaning in this town hall for twenty years, and I don't need a cheeky brat like you asking me where I come from. So now get out before I really lose my temper!«

Instinctively, Jennifer took a step back.

headscarf: das Kopftuch

impertinence: die Unverschämtheit

»Are – are there any more of you outside?« stammered Ben. He was really talking to himself more than anything, but the woman had heard what he said.
She waved her scrubbing brush threateningly in the air. »Don't you answer back like that or you'll be sorry, young man!« she said crossly. »I'm going to call the town hall night watchmen. They'll teach you manners. Now then, tell me where your teacher is, so he can take the whole lot of you away!«
»They're back! The grown-ups are back! We're back!« shouted Frank, running past the cleaning lady, through the door and out. The other twenty children immediately ran after him. The old woman jumped aside in alarm, dropped her bucket, and the water went over her feet. She staggered back, slipped in the soapy water, tripped on her scrubbing brush and fell to the floor, screeching out loud.
»Sorry!« muttered Thomas, trotting out of the room past the woman on the floor, last as usual.
The children ran out into the street and stood there, astonished.
There was a traffic jam in the High Street, with lots of cars hooting their horns. Pedestrians were hurrying past the shops with grumpy expressions. A bus driver was just closing the bus doors in an old lady's face, and drove off grinning. Two tramps sat by the fountain, begging from passers by. A dog was doing its business right by the lights at the pedestrian

crossing, while its owner looked in the air as if the dog was nothing to do with him. Two policemen were standing by a snack stall eating sausages.
»We're back in our own world!« said Miriam.
»And now I want to find out how things are at home,« said Frank. »See you all at school tomorrow!« He was about to run off, but he suddenly stopped abruptly. »I've just thought of something,« he said, turning to Ben. »I don't think I've earned your tracksuit for this **frightful** game. I'll give it back to you tomorrow. Only you must promise never, never to run the game again.«

frightful: furchtbar

Ben smiled at his friend. »I certainly won't,« he promised. Next moment, however, his face froze. »The game!« he cried. »It's still in the golden computer! Suppose someone else tries running it?«
He was about to turn and race back to the mayor's office, but Thomas stopped him. »Don't panic!« Thomas grinned. »I thought no one was going to need that CD any more, so I took it. Because the great thing about stuff you find isn't whether you need it or not . . .«
». . . but it's for free and you only have to pick it up!« cried the other children in unison, hugging Thomas the famous collector. He grinned broadly.
»Oh, Thomas,« said Ben. »What would we do without you? But take good care of that game. We don't want anyone else to find it, ever.«
»Nobody except me can find anything at all in my ga-

rage,« Thomas assured him. All the others knew that only too well.
»Right,« cried Frank. »Now I really do have to find out what's going on at home. Bye, see you tomorrow.« And he sprinted off as if competing for the European hundred metres championship. The others wanted to go home, too. They said goodbye to each other and disappeared in all directions, taking the shortest possible way home.

Ben rushed through the front door into the hall.
»Mum, are you there?« he called. His mother put her head around the kitchen door.
»Hi, Ben. Well, you really are home on the dot today! We can eat straight . . .« But she never finished her sentence. Ben made for his mother and flung his arms around her.
»Oh, Mum!« he cried. »It's great to have you back!«
»Well, that's a nice thing to say!« said his mother in surprise. »Have you been up to something?«
»Up to something?« asked Ben indignantly. »You've been away for a week. All of you were away for a week. Or rather, well, really I was away for a week. I mean we were away for a week! I'm just so glad to see you again!«
»Aren't you feeling well?« Ben's mother began to feel anxious about her son. What kind of nonsense was he talking? »What do you mean, you were away for a week?«

»But you must have noticed!« said Ben desperately. »All you grown-ups disappeared. Though really it was us, the kids, who disappeared. Into Kid City!«
»Ben, that will do,« his mother told him. »What's this nonsense all about?«
Ben realized that his mother obviously really didn't know anything about it. He began telling her the story, getting excited and very mixed up. She listened **incredulously** as she put supper on the table. It was six by now, which meant supper time. Ben had no appetite at all. »Well, so here we finally are, back a week later!« he finished his story.

incredulously: ungläubig

»Oh yes?« said his mother. »And who was the boy who left so early for school and in such a hurry because the best of all computer games was waiting for him?« she asked.
»This morning?« cried Ben. »It wasn't this morning, it was a week ago!«
»Ben,« said his mother, in a very serious tone now. »I really don't know if sitting around all afternoon in front of the computer is good for you. Now you're beginning to get your games confused with real life. Do eat your supper. I bought some really fresh cauliflower in the shopping centre, and I know how much you like it.«
»Oh, Mum. Please, you have to believe me. It was . . .«
But Ben was stopped short in mid-sentence by the phone ringing.
Ben's mother answered the phone. »For you,« she said. »Jennifer.«

(to) **sob**: schluchzen

exasperation: die Verzweiflung

Ben took the receiver.

»Ben, my parents won't believe me!« Jennifer wailed. »I told them everything, but they only laugh, and now they want to take me to a movie just as if nothing had happened! What am I to do? Couldn't you have a word with them and explain it?«

»I'm afraid not,« said Ben sadly. »It's the same here.« He paused for a moment, and heard Jennifer **sobbing** at the other end of the line. »Hold on a moment,« he said at last. He put the receiver to one side and went into the kitchen. »Listen, Mum. Did you just say you'd bought cauliflower from the *shopping centre*? Er – didn't you notice anything there?«

»Of course,« replied his mother. »The price of vegetables has risen again. If this goes on . . .«

Ben rolled his eyes in **exasperation** and interrupted his mother. »I mean hadn't anything been smashed up in there? No broken windows, no tomatoes on the walls, no fish on the floor?«

»No, why? Is something supposed to have happened there?«

Ben sprinted back to the phone receiver. »Jennifer!« he called into it. »Did you notice anything on the way home?«

»Notice anything?« said Jennifer thoughtfully. »No, what was there to notice? It was all the same as ever.«

»The same as ever or the same as last week?«

»The same as before the computer game. The grown-ups were back again and . . . wait a minute! I've only just thought of something!«
»What?«
»The bar, the drugstore! You said they were burnt down. I had to pass them on the way home, and they were all there as usual!«
»That's what I thought,« groaned Ben.
»How come?«
»The computer game is over. And like all computer games, once it's finished it goes back to the beginning so you can play it again. And then everything's the way it was before. So the bar isn't burnt down, the shopping centre's intact, and everything at school will be back to normal, too. Nothing. No sign of our week away.«
»You mean . . .« Jennifer began.
Ben answered at once. »Yes, I mean it's one hundred per cent certain no one will believe us. No one knows what happened except us children.«
»And what adult ever did believe a child?« added Jennifer gloomily.
»Ben, do come along!« called his mother from the kitchen. »Supper's getting cold. If you go on like this you can start getting your own supper tomorrow, and then you'll know how much trouble it is.«
Jennifer had heard that over the phone. »Ask her if she's ever made noodles and tomato sauce for over a hundred children,« she **chuckled**.

(to) chuckle: kichern

Ben had to laugh. »Yes, besides putting out the fire in two burning buildings!« he added.
They both burst out laughing down the phone. Then Jennifer suddenly turned serious. »Listen, Ben. If it's all back to the way it was, then the mayor's plan is back in his office, and Miriam nicking it did no good at all.«
»That's right.« Ben thought of that now, too. »But we won't let them take the sports field away so easily, I can tell you that.«
»What will you do about it?« asked Jennifer.
»No idea yet, but between us all we're sure to think of something. I found that out last week!«
»You're right,« agreed Jennifer, not without pride. »I'm afraid I have to go now,« she said. »My parents are taking me to see a movie. *The Jungle Book*. I really wanted to see *The Lord of the Rings*, but they think it's too old for me.«
»I can see why,« Ben teased her. »But if your parents ever have trouble with a gang of boys running wild, they can always turn to you for help.«
(to) crow: jauchzen
Jennifer **crowed** with delight. »You mean a gang with a certain leader called Kolya?«
»Exactly!« said Ben. »Okay, Jennifer, you go off to the movie, and I'll eat my cauliflower. We'll act like good little kids. And tomorrow we'll start thinking about the sports field.«
»Fine,« said Jennifer. »Tell you what, Ben, though – why don't we go and see *The Lord of the Rings* together tomorrow?«

»Good idea!« **beamed** Ben. »Okay, and then we'll start thinking about the sports field the next day!«
»Great!« said Jennifer happily. »Hey, Ben – I like you.«
»I like you, too,« whispered Ben. Then he hung up, went into the kitchen and ate his cauliflower.
»At last!« said Ben's mother. »The idea of having to look after yourself for a few days scared you a bit, right?«
»Well, no,« said Ben. »But sometimes I'm really glad you're here to look after me and I'm only thirteen.«

Smiling, Ben's mother shook her head. What would her son take into his head next?

(to) beam: strahlen